Dragons

Dragons

A Handbook of History & Lore
from Basilisks to Wyverns

Agnes Hollyhock

castle

Contents

Introduction

Where does one begin to unfold the legends surrounding dragons, and how does one tie the creature as we know it now to the myths that gave the fantasy meaning? The modern world depicts dragons in a variety of ways, all of which we very clearly define as "fiction." But were there times in the past where dragons were more than something dreamed up and sculpted in the minds of artists? Potentially. Were they ever truly believed in, or were they only believed in earnest by the utterly gullible and/or hopeful? It's difficult to say.

Modern dragons often evoke a very specific image: a large winged (although sometimes not) reptile with a nigh impenetrable scaly hide armed with claws, a powerful tail, and immense intelligence. Archetypes and breeds of dragons may change, and their abilities and objectives shift—especially from one work of fiction to another—but when someone says the word "dragon," whoever they are talking to will have a general idea of what they're talking about.

This is because dragons are now the ultimate creature in fantasy. These large megafauna cryptids evoke imagery of castles, treasure hoards, and damsels in distress. In medieval literature and folklore, slaying a dragon was the ultimate test of a knight's virtue and strength, and avoiding getting roasted was a testament to their cunning. Medieval European folklore painted dragons as dastardly monsters made of sin. But Western mythology is not the only origin for dragons. Countless other cultures have myths and legends regarding dragons or dragon-like creatures.

Eastern cultures align dragons with luck and tie them to the life-giving powers of large bodies of water and rivers. An aboriginal creation myth paints a dragon as a key character in what gave the world life. Some dragons are akin to divine gods and goddesses, while others are no more than a zoological beast found in the far-flung areas of the globe. Throughout history, they've been depicted in a variety of ways: strong symbols and metaphors; real-life creatures to

be feared, hunted, or tamed; sinful shapeshifters that prey on women and livestock; deities that can either give life to the cosmos or rule the dead in the underworld; and starved monsters of immeasurable carnage.

While all life started as one cell in the sea, it is tempting to think that there must be some common denominator that inspired the global population to believe in such an unbelievable monster. Dinosaurs, perhaps? The amalgamation of all humanity's earliest predators to create a "bogeyman" of sorts? The mysterious missing link of all dragonkind has yet to be found (and may not even exist), but that does not stop people from dreaming up new dragons.

Dragons continue to burn through our collective conscious—we love a story with a dragon, cultures across time have identified with the beast's power, and we allow only our most prolific role models to carry the mantle of "Dragon." Modern dragons are a sum of their history—centuries of context have weighed in on the way today's audiences see and interpret dragons. Sift through the myths and legends within these pages to slake any curiosity regarding dragon origins. Delve into the caves of forgotten texts and find untold treasures in their history. Dragons are fascinating creatures, whether they are earnestly believed in or viewed as purely creatures of fiction. Their past is storied, diverse, and carries curious ties across cultures.

Dive in and be warned, *here there be dragons.*

The Origins of Dragons

Which came first, the dragon or its egg? Dragons have emerged as early as antiquity (human history that occurred before the Middle Ages) in cultures across the globe. This chapter will explore how each iteration of the dragon arose and the earliest instances of humans believing in dragons and dragon-like creatures. While it is impossible to know for sure what our ancient ancestors were thinking, we can consider the possibilities of how these ancient humans came up with the idea of a dragon in the first place.

❖ ❖ ❖

WHAT TO KNOW ABOUT DRAGONS

Dragons are marvelous fantasy beasts that appear in just about every culture. Much of the information in this book draws upon history, folklore, and a bit of modern archaeology and anthropology. Many of the same elements pop up in cultures across continents. Some aspects of dragons are relatively fixed, while others are unique to a singular dragon or a privileged few. These quirks make the creatures distinct to the culture in which they appear.

Before we get started, there are a few key terms that will come up in this book and defining them will be beneficial going forward.

✿ **Saurian:** Refers to any large reptile or describing something reptilian. Dinosaurs and dragons in this book are *saurian*.

✿ **Antiquity:** The antiquity period of human society stretches from the earliest civilizations (dating back to as early as 6000–4000 BCE) to the beginning of the Middle Ages (which began 475 CE). The earliest recorded references of dragons come from antiquity.

✿ **Middle Ages:** The Middle Ages (475–1500) was the time when dragons were most prevalent. As people's understanding of the geography of the world grew, dragons began to worm their way in along the edges. It is difficult to decipher if during this time people genuinely believed in dragons, approached them with heavy skepticism, or understood them to be a symbol for something other than an enormous reptile.

❖ ❖ ❖

- **Modern Era:** The Modern Era follows the Middle Ages and spans from 1500 to 1945. This time period was an age of industrial and political revolution. As the edges of the map of the world filled in, there were less places for dragons to hide other than in ancient myths. A select few people sought out dragon-like creatures, and the field of paleontology and fossil hunting began in this period. Dragon sightings were more scattered than they had been in the Middle Ages.

- **Contemporary Period:** From 1945 until the present day, humanity's belief in winged saurians has diminished to fringe sciences. Certain cryptids still make the news, but are rarely, if ever, taken seriously.

WHERE DID THEY COME FROM?

The roots of many dragons in mythology are hard to trace. Heinz Mode—a German historian, anthropologist, and archaeologist from the 1970s—suggested that monster myths (like dragons) began when primitive peoples developed into early cultures in antiquity. If this is true, the belief in certain dragon gods could be as old as human culture itself. In fact, some appear in ancient religions as gods and others appear to evolve from a nearby culture's myth.

As people came to know more of the world, there are certain representations that define what it means to be a dragon by today's standard. When humanity was young, however, there was a wealth of different types of dragons.

Regionally, dragons all hold a similar shape. North American dragons are largely horned or plumed serpents. European dragons are winged, scaled saurians that are usually depicted as being malicious and evil. Serpentine Asian dragons all usually have short legs, no wings, and a strong connection to water and clouds. Many coastal communities and sailors have told stories of enormous serpents that wrestle whales and keep pace with their ship.

But what was the first dragon? And why are there so many across the globe? Cultural exchange can be partially credited, but the deepest origins of these beasts are likely rooted in fossils and tales of live lizards.

Fossils

At the intersection of anthropology, paleontology, and archaeology lies the belief that dragons and other mythical creatures were originally created by the people of antiquity to explain away ancient remains. Many fossil dig sites overlap with well-known origins of mythological beasts.

For example, mammoth skulls have a giant hole in the center of their face for their trunk. Ancient Greeks would likely be unfamiliar with elephants, and finding a fossilized mammoth skull would be quite a baffling discovery. The trunk hole in a mammoth skull could very well look like a single eye socket for a giant creature, such as the Greek Cyclops. Known locations in myths with cyclops overlap with those of deposits of mammoth fossils.

Additionally, the griffin is a mythological creature that has a bird's head and lion's body. While prominent in Greek mythology, the origins for the beast come from the Gobi Desert in Mongolia, which is rife with fossils of small four-legged triceratops with beaks in their nests. Ancient people examining the skeletons and nests likely speculated the creature's anatomy and came up with griffins.

Fossils were considered "dragon bones" in Traditional Chinese Medicine (TCM), and when fossil-hunting became popular in the 1800s, Chinese apothecaries and their guarded sources were key to finding large fossil deposits in China. These sources also illuminated another interesting connection between fossils and dragons. In Asian cultures, dragons are strongly linked to large bodies. Sedimentary rock, a common environment for fossils, is formed by water passing over rock for long periods of time. Unearthing fossils in riverbeds, especially those of unknown reptiles, could be some of humanity's earliest inspiration for dragons.

Crocodiles and Monitor Lizards

Living dinosaurs, like crocodiles and monitor lizards, could also be the source of some dragon mythology, particularly what emerged in the Middle Ages. Strange tales of exotic beasts in far-flung places were coveted by those who lived exclusively in their small slice of the world. Like a game of telephone, as stories of these creatures spread, their descriptions changed and took on new forms.

Marco Polo (1254–1324) was an Italian merchant and trader that traversed the Silk Road, a legendary trade route between Europe and Asia. He became famous by romanticizing his travels and transforming his journals of the experience into a book: *The Travels of Marco Polo*. In it, he dazzles the reader with accounts of the exotic people,

Komodo Dragon

The Komodo dragon is a monitor lizard from select islands in Indonesia that is so large that it has been colloquially dubbed a dragon. They're independent hunters with sedating saliva that helps them take down prey, even prey that are larger than themselves. Thus their spit, look, and hunting style make them real-life dragons!

places, and creatures he saw. Two mythical creatures well-known by today's standards make an appearance in the pages of Polo's account: the unicorn and the dragon. The unicorn he spotted in Indonesia is described as having a black horn, loving mud, and being very ugly and unpleasant (because he was describing a rhinoceros). Likewise, the "dragons" he described in China were low to the ground and slunk towards watering holes to hunt. Based on the location and how the trappers caught these dragons, they were likely small alligators. Historians now know that Marco Polo had a habit of grossly embellishing to improve the story quality of his travels. Back then though, his book was a bestseller.

Large Snakes

There are only three types of snakes that are native to the United Kingdom, yet to this day, nearly half of the people in the UK are afraid of snakes. Anacondas (native to South America), boa constrictors (also native to South America), and pythons (found in Africa, India, the Indochina peninsula, and Australia) are enormous serpents found in warm climates. At their largest, they've been logged to weigh up to five hundred pounds (227 kg) and have grown to nearly 30 feet (9 m) long. Imagine how powerful and fearsome any of these creatures would have appeared to those who had only seen the scant three UK types in their lifetimes.

Another excellent example of how extra-continental telephone works: the amphisbaena is a dragon-like creature described as having two legs and two heads, with its second head attached to the end of its tail. This is likely inspired by a real ancient lizard in Libya (the amphisbaena's purported habitat), which would run with their tail in the air to give the appearance of being a snake ready to strike. This poisonous creature was perpetuated by many a medieval bestiary.

EARLIEST RECORDS OF DRAGONS

The dragons in early myths are less like gods and more like physical forces of nature. Most of them are large serpents rather than the winged quadrupeds that dominate modern dragon imagery, with some exceptions. These creatures are both devious devourers of souls and benevolent bringers of life-giving water. What follows is a broad view of the earliest records of when dragons slithered out alongside human culture.

Australia (Potentially 6000 BCE)

Dreamtime mythology, which is a broad term that covers spiritual beliefs of many Native Australian cultures, has a few versions of the Rainbow Serpent. These creatures are deeply connected to water and will hibernate in the mud during times of drought. They can either be monstrous mythic beasts or intelligent spiritual creatures, if not malevolent spirits. The Yolngu's version of Dreamtime mythology's great Rainbow Serpent is named Yulunggu, and he lives in deep water pools and floods the world when he's displeased. He also devoured some of the first humans whole only to be shamed into coughing them up.

❖ ❖ ❖

While early written records of this creature are difficult, if not impossible, to come by, some of the cave paintings and ancient archaeological sites associated with it potentially date back as early as 6000 BCE.

Chinese Jade Dragons (4500–3000 BCE)

China has always had a strong connection to dragons. The earliest written record of dragons was *Shan Hai Jing*, which translates to *The Classic of Mountains and Seas*. This text as we know it today was likely compiled over several centuries, with the earlier portions associated with Chinese Taoism likely being written sometime between 400 and 200 BCE. Much of it was compiled during the Han Dynasty (206 BCE–220 CE), with some portions likely written around the first century BCE.

Draco Constellation

Latin for dragon, Draco's serpentine constellation is heavily associated with ancient Greek mythology. It is said to be from when Athena killed a dragon and threw it in the sky, where it writhed in pain before it froze. It could also be Ladon, the dragon slain by Hercules (who slew *a lot* of dragons) while guarding Hera's golden apples, who was immortalized by Hera in the sky after Ladon's defeat.

While this written record is quite impressive, there is earlier evidence still. Certain archaeological sites in Wuhan, China, where the Hongshan people carved small jade "dragon pigs," date back to sometime between 4500 and 3000 BCE.

Ancient Egypt and Ancient Greece (3000–1782 BCE)

The Ancient Egyptian serpentine god of chaos and darkness, Apep, or Apophis in ancient Greek (see page 92), is one of the earliest dragon-like deities in the ancient world. The earliest reference to Apep is in the Egyptian *Book of the Dead*, dating back to sometime between 2040 and 1782 BCE.

Predating that book are the Pyramid Texts written on the walls of ancient pyramids. These inscriptions included nefarious giant serpents that could have been earlier, unnamed versions of Apep or other dragon-like creatures. It is commonly believed that the Pyramid texts were written as early as 3000 BCE.

Mesopotamia (2334–2150 BCE)

The area known as Mesopotamia in the Middle East is the cradle of human civilization, with several early civilizations emerging in the same area. First were the Sumerians, who arose sometime around 2900 BCE. They existed alongside the Akkadians, who coalesced as early as 2340 BCE. Finally, Babylonian society began as early as 1800 BCE, concurrent with the earlier Akkadians and Sumerians.

These three cultures have overlapping pantheons of gods, myths, and legends. One prominent dragon in these mythologies is the chaotic draconic creation goddess Tiâmat (see page 213). There are anti-magic hymns in old Akkadian from 2334 to 2154 BCE that protect against Tiâmat specifically. Tiâmat's defeat was mentioned in the *Epic of Gilgamesh*, which can be dated from stone slabs to sometime between 1780 and 514 BCE.

Vedic Texts in India (1500–1000 BCE)

According to Spanish Bishop Isidore of Seville (ca. 560–636 CE), India was the birthplace of dragons, and he may have been right! The *Rig Veda*, a book of Sanskrit hymns written sometime between 1500 and 1200 BCE, describes the fearsome dragon, Vritra (see page 116), that stole all the water of the earth and had to be slain by the storm god, Indra, to release life-giving water back to humans. There are also other serpent-deities and demigods in Indian mythology, each with ancient origins. Many of these deities are connected to water and monsoons, following the trend of ancient prehistoric dragons holding dominion over the forces of water.

Old and New Testament Dragons (1200 BCE–300 CE)

The Old Testament was likely written between 1200–100 BCE; the New Testament sometime between 100 and 300 CE. Fearsome monsters and miraculous events occur plentifully in both the Old and New Testament, which are important to both Judaism and Christianity.

Dragons appear in both the Old and New Testaments, with the oldest draconic creature being Leviathan, the enormous and chaotic sea serpent (see page 102) from *The Book of Isaiah* in the Old Testament. The Great Red Dragon (see page 97) from the New Testament kicks off the end of the world in *Revelation*. While both are described as dragons, Leviathan is more of a serpent, whereas the Great Red Dragon typically replicates what we think of, by modern standards, as European dragons.

Other instances of dragons occur as well—dragons are numerous around the Tower of Babel. One biblical hero, Daniel, even slays the dragon god in Babylon.

American Stone Stelas (1200–500 BCE)

The oldest dragons in the Americas are plumed serpents. The Olmecs, Mayans, and Aztecs all had a relatively similar plumed serpent god of the wind. The Olmecs worshipped this deity first, as is evident by stone stelas (or carved upright stone slabs) that still exist to this day. No written records survive, but archaeologists' best guess is that the plumed serpent was most popular sometime between 1200 and 500 BCE. After the Olmecs, the Mayans worshipped the plumed

Humble Hypothesis

One theory as to why there are so many dragons across different cultures is that dragons are a superpredator—an amalgamation of all the main predators of our ancient primate ancestors. It was imperative that early primates alerted their entire family group to these predators such as hawks or flying raptors, large carnivorous cats, and poisonous reptiles, or else have their numbers decimated. The ones who were keenly alert to the signs of these three predators would survive. The remnants of our ancient primate brains would create a shortcut—a combination of these three creatures that would put ancient humans into a high-alert fight-or-flight mode to ensure their survival.

From hawks, eagles, and other flying raptors, dragons were bestowed flight, feathers, and razor-sharp talons. From large cats, their quiet hunter's inclination, a terrifying roar, large maw of teeth, four legs, and intimidating size. From snakes, a deadly threat from their mouth, shining scales, and whip-like tail. Put together, rough versions of dragons as they appear in their original forms feature across antiquity.

While this theory is curious and compelling, there is little concrete evidence to support it.

❖ ❖ ❖

serpent as Kukulkan, after which the Aztecs worshipped him as Quetzalcoatl, which is the most well-known name of the deity to date.

HOW FOLKLORE GREW

Dragon sightings were at their peak in the Middle Ages. This was a period of increasing connectivity and discovery for a traveled few, while many people stayed rooted in their communities. Stories of far-off lands and a desire to know more about those areas inspired great curiosity. A desire to catalogue the unknown, know the unknowable, and tell their stories inspired tales that walked the line of something believed as truth or understood as allegory.

While many scholarly texts cite dragons as residing in novel areas of the globe, they likely got their beginnings in local folklore. Two types of people were integral in keeping folklore alive and spreading it far and wide.

Monks and Scholars

While not intrinsically linked in folklore, monks are a key reason for why we know as much about dragons as we do. Christian monasteries in the Middle Ages had chroniclers who kept a record of the goings-on in the area. They were usually most interested in recording things that could protect the monastery. Medieval dragon sightings were considered important because dragons were an omen for something terrible.

Monks also gathered and shared information from their ancient history (the period we know as antiquity) and disseminated it amongst other monasteries. For example, writings by Ancient Roman author and naturalist Pliny the Elder and Ancient Greek historian Herodotus approached dragons with an academic lens and acted as source material for aspiring historical writers in the Middle Ages. Thus, it's unclear whether dragons were thought to be real (albeit exotic, rather than commonplace), mythical, or if they were considered creatures of the past.

Bards

Bards are authors, historians, and musicians dedicated to preserving folklore and culture through the retelling of stories. Whether they be songs, sagas, or epics, bards ensured that local lore lived on. In oral traditions, characters and plots may change between different areas. Bards collected stories to preserve their culture and to capture the most interesting narratives that would garner the largest audience.

Stories collected and retold by bards would grow and change as bards traveled. While the stories they knew largely hit all the same beats across different areas, embellishments and tweaks to tales might be made if people in certain places had strong connections to the land. Bards were common in medieval Europe. One example is Snorri Sturluson, the author of *The Prose Edda* that describes Norse mythology in detail. Another excellent example of a bard tale is *The Classic of Mountains and Seas* from China, which not only tells of the mythical creatures in many parts of China but also serves as a list of landmarks per area across the large land mass.

❖ ❖ ❖

Dragon Lore

The mythology of dragons across the globe is rich, and the folklore that it evolved into is just as layered. In certain places, the mythology and folklore surrounding dragons are woven together like two serpents spiraling into the sky. The lore and stories in this chapter are by no means exhaustive but cover the more widely known and intriguing dragon tales.

A BROAD VIEW OF DRAGONS IN FOLKLORE AND MYTHOLOGY

Mythology and folklore are types of narratives that are intricately linked. Sometimes, they are used interchangeably, and while there are examples where a lore can be considered both, it isn't always so.

We often refer to anything regarding religious tales and religious sacred texts as being part of that religion's mythology. There is an official air to anything that is labeled a myth: the governing holy entity has stamped these stories with their seal of approval.

Folklore refers to stories shared by word-of-mouth and expanded upon by people who aren't part of the hierarchy of organized religion—the folk, as it were. Folktales often have many different iterations, as is the nature of being told and retold by many different people who want to expand and embellish whatever story they are telling.

The line between folklore and mythology is murky since both rely on the belief of people and often enforce some sort of moral teaching, but it does exist. The line in the mud is that mythology is accepted canon of a religion, and folklore are stories meant to entertain and sometimes teach. Otherwise, mythology can be told in folktales, and folklore can be written down. Some folktales are exalted to the status of myth to help capture people's attention, often as an attempt to sway them to a new religion. Likewise, beloved mythological features, creatures, and tales will often be expanded into a network of folktales.

Chapter 1 focused on the history and origins of dragons, and thus much of what was explained there is considered "mythology," especially when the dragon in question is a god or goddess. This chapter explores the shifting and evolving mythology behind dragons, as well as various folklore beliefs that sprung up when dragons took hold of people's imaginations.

European Dragon Lore

Many of the myths and legends from different European cultures (Nordic, Celtic, Illyrian, Germanic, and Cantabrian, to name a few) cast dragons as malevolent, fire-breathing beasts that sowed chaos and destruction. It is hard to say whether the dragons from these cultures were

Dragonfly

A dragonfly's long spindly form and delicate translucent wings that rest perpendicular to its body don't necessarily evoke the same imagery of majestic dragons, but it is a ferocious aerial hunter in the insect world. There are hundreds of species of dragonflies across the globe, and they have names that translate to "Devil's Horse," "Devil's Fly," and "Magic Spindle" in other languages.

always represented as such. As Christian abbeys spread across Europe, monks began earnestly keeping records of the history and folklore of different areas, putting their own spin on the regional folktales in the process. Monks would consolidate histories, legends, and other bits of scavenged information from the accounts of explorers, traders, locals, ancient texts, other scholars, and warriors alike.

One such prolific writer, Spanish Bishop Isidore of Seville, created the gold standard of classical knowledge at the time, titled *Etymologies*. In it, he described all manner of histories and natural sciences in what could be called one of the world's first encyclopedias. This epic tome describes dragons as creatures from Ethiopia and India that thrive in scalding climates rather than monsters local to Europe.

Etymologies is also a template for a popular series of books that contributed to dragon lore in the Middle Ages: *bestiaries*. Medieval European bestiaries would explain local and exotic fauna, often in a way that was meant to fascinate and entertain. Representations in these tomes claimed that dragons existed in Africa or India (likely due to Bishop Seville's influence) and morally aligned the creatures with evil.

Bishop Seville's work is an excellent representation of how European dragon lore in the Middle Ages (from around 450–1450 CE, depending on the scholar you ask) inspired contemporary ideas about dragons. Bishops, monks, and other holy record keepers labeled dragons as agents of the devil. In fact, the language the Torah and the Bible use to describe the snake in the Garden of Eden is also used to

Arthur Pendragon

The legend of King Arthur Pendragon and associated Arthurian legends are rife with fantasy mainstays: a wizard, a witch, a magical sword, talking animals, and—although a startling lack considering the king's surname—dragons.

The sixth- and seventh-century Welsh poetry that Arthurian legends come from does not neatly assign him the last name "Pendragon." Rather, Pendragon is a title, meaning "head dragon" or "chief dragon," with "dragon," in context, meaning war leader. Other translations poetically interpret Pendragon to mean "the dragon's head," which aligns with the fact that Arthur was the leader of a military force, and there are historical reports of an Arthur Pendragon winning battles.

The earliest written records of King Arthur are in the Welsh Annals compiled sometime around 830 BCE. Notably, the earliest recorded dragons associated with Arthurian legends rear their scaly heads long before Arthur is even born. As a young boy, the wizard Merlin divines a prophecy foretelling the end of an independent Wales based on the outcome of a battle between a red dragon and a white dragon.

Later works in the Arthurian canon include the knight Lancelot fighting a dragon on his quest for the Holy Grail, as well as the knight Tristan fighting a dragon. The dragons in earlier legends represent the might of a nation. As time passed, dragons transformed from a symbol of the people to an obstacle to be defeated by virtuous knights.

describe monstrous dragons, with Satan himself sometimes described as a dragon. From there, tales and epic poetry emerged about the knights in Arthurian legends showing their mettle by besting dragons, and the thought of righteous knights fighting dragons during the crusades as part of their holy rite gained popularity.

Whether or not medieval European peasants or monks genuinely believed that dragons existed remains a mystery, but the scholarly dedication of Bishop Seville implies that at least a few people thought devilish dragons stalked the cliffs, caves, and crags of the world.

American Dragon Lore

Historically, dragons in the Americas have most prominently been represented by the same two gods or godlike beings in a variety of iterations. In Mesoamerica, a plumed serpent appears across ancient art and belief systems. The plumed serpent began with Olmec artistic renditions sometime between 1500 and 400 BCE, evolved into the Mayan Kukulkan, and ended as a creator god Quetzalcoatl, responsible for life and death in the Aztec pantheon.

In North America, the Great Horned Serpent appears in the folktales of many different Native American tribes, with each iteration being unique. Some Horned Serpents are mindless monsters that lurk in deep waters while others steal wives and can take the form of a man. The Hopi, Seminole, Zuni, Shawnee, and Cherokee tribes all have a horned serpent in their mythology. It is unlikely that these

❖ ❖ ❖

different horned serpents all came from a single source, but North American dragons are likely based on a healthy fear and respect for snakes.

Other notable dragons are a slew of sea monster sightings along the east and west coasts in the early 1800s.

Asian Dragon Myths

Asian dragon myths borrow and share a lot of lore from different countries. Many of the dragons in coastal cultures (such as China, Korea, Japan, Vietnam, and others) have similar depictions. They are serpentine, scaled, four-legged creatures that can fly, are strongly tied to large bodies of water, and have at least some modicum of control over the weather. Dragon Kings (see page 126) rule over the lesser dragons and are in charge of distributing rainfall. Dragon Kings can often shapeshift into stunningly beautiful humans. They live in magnificent castles under the waves and gather vast amounts of magical items and treasures.

Dragons are powerful and meaningful creatures in Asian mythology, often tied to creation, divinity, life-giving water, and imperial rule.

Pacific Dragon Myths

Oceania and Pacific islands contain a lot of cosmic serpents that were present at the beginning of the universe. Some of them are gods among reptiles, but more often than not, these cosmic or celestial serpents are infinite in their reach. Much like dragons in Indian and other Asian cultures, Oceanic and Pacific dragons tend to be tied to water.

In Australia, the Rainbow Serpent floods land when it's angry and hops from pool to pool via a rainbow. In Malaysian mythology, an enormous serpent locally known as naga (which is not quite the same as the Indian naga on page 133), is responsible for the creation of freshwater lakes. In Indonesia, ancient Javanese people believed in a celestial snake called Antaboga that created the universe.

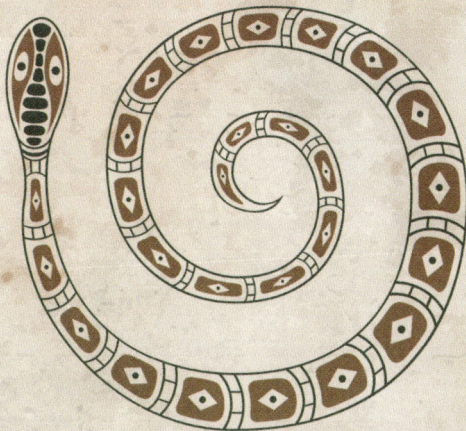

African Dragon Myths

Serpent mythology in Africa is robust and diverse. In addition to Apep (see page 92), serpents, crocodiles, and other dragon-like creatures were common in ancient Egyptian mythology. An old creature of chaos and darkness, Apep attempts to swallow the sun god, Ra, during his nightly sojourn through the underworld. In vivid contrast to the darkness of Apep, the Dahomey people of West Africa believed in a Rainbow Serpent called Aido Hwedo (see page 90) that was present at the creation of the universe.

Several historical accounts from the Classical Era (between 500 BCE and 500 CE) make note of small yet vicious winged serpents in Ancient Egypt and Arabia (what is now known as the Middle East). Famed ancient Greek historian, Herodotus, went in search of these creatures that supposedly had mating rituals that resulted in both parents perishing before their offspring were born (the mother would devour the father, and the offspring would eat their way out of the mother), and were also consumed by flocks of black ibises (a heron-like bird) in droves.

Africa is one of the places that medieval bestiaries described as the birthplace of dragons. This was perpetuated by a tale of Saint George, who rescues a princess (in what is modern day Ethiopia) from being sacrificed to a dragon to protect her people. This may be based off a creature in African mythology called Bida, from modern-day Ghana, that would demand a sacrifice of maidens in exchange for gold.

Indian Dragon Myths

Along with Vritra, India has a few other dragons associated with their mythology. The naga (see page 133) are important draconic figures. Nagas bridge the gap between the benevolent dragons of the East and the wrathful dragons of the West. These half-human, half-serpent creatures protect powerful gods and viciously battle with their enemies. There is a strong connection among the Vritra, the nagas, and the Chinese lóng, which was likely the result of a cultural exchange that transformed all the creatures into what we recognize today.

While not originating from India itself, many medieval European sources on dragons earnestly advocated for the existence of dragons in India. Edward Topsell (1572–1625 CE), a revered medieval English clergyman and bestiary author, wrote of how Alexander the Great (a Macedonian king and conqueror from 400 to 300 BCE) encountered a dragon in India that was so massive, it could not be viewed in its entirety. Topsell's account states that the people there worshipped this sacred dragon and fed it several sheep and oxen a day. Illuminated manuscripts with Alexander the Great and dragons in the margins were not uncommon in European literature of the Middle Ages. Topsell also described Indian dragons as being yellow with shining scales, ridged-back monsters with beards and strong snouts.

Middle Eastern Dragon Myths

While the earliest dragons in the area are Tiâmat and Kur, the Middle East has a strong mythology surrounding dragons. Persian folklore was also rich in dragons. One

❖ ❖ ❖

Dragon Chess

Dragon chess was invented by Gary Gygax, the creator of Dungeons & Dragons. The game involves playing chess across three platforms with thirteen types of pieces. The three levels of the board represent the sky, ground, and underground. The goal of dragon chess is the same as regular chess, which is to topple the king.

curious Persian myth involves the legendary hero, Rostam, and his horse Rakash.

Rostam was given several monumental tasks (very much like the Labors of Hercules, see page 39), and while he rested in between duties, his horse Rakash would stand watch. The horse was intelligent, with keen eyesight, and noticed a dragon lurking just beyond camp. Rakash woke up Rostam three times, and each time the dragon hid, making it seem as if the horse was playing a prank on his rider rather than warning him of a very serious danger. The third time, Rostam—at the end of his wits— threatened to assault the horse if he roused him again without reason. Afraid of both his master's fury and the wrath of a dragon, the horse persisted, and this time God illuminated the fiendish creature so that Rakash would be believed. Astride Rakash, the two took down the beast, partially thanks to Rakash taking a hefty bite of the dragon, which was so out of character it startled both his rider and the monster.

Sea Serpents

The oldest recordings of enormous sea serpents are likely Leviathan (see page 102), Jormungandr (see page 98), and Kur (see page 100). However, there are also plenty of tales of fishermen spotting sea dragons. Multiple eyewitness accounts across history and around globe claim to have seen sea serpents ranging from thirty to two hundred feet (9 to 61 m) long. Reports frequently described them as being black with red eyes, and occasionally lifting their massive heads out of the water to tower over seafaring vessels. They were said to be able to swim incredibly fast and would sometimes shoot geysers of water from their mouths. Many people (both modern and at the times of the

Hercules (Greece)

Hercules, a demigod, is best known in Greek mythology for his Twelve Labors, or trials that he faced as punishment for being tricked into murdering his family by the jealous goddess Hera. A prolific dragon slayer in Greek mythology, two of his twelve labors were to slay dragon-like creatures—the many-headed Lernean hydra (see page 98) and the dragon Ladon (see page 19) that guarded Hera's golden apples.

sighting) speculate that what the sailors actually saw were most likely partial views of various types of whales. Claims of sea serpents were widely published in the 1800s. This was also the century that the first paleontologists arose, meaning that several ancient dinosaurs with skeletons that looked very much like fearsome sea dragons became popular museum exhibits.

FOLKLORE PAIRINGS

As dragons became popular creatures for myths and stories, certain tropes would continually appear. Dragons are meant to be slain by folk heroes; they're the easy adversary in a story. Dragons and maidens dance around themes of corruption. Emperors draw on dragons' strength. And magic runs in the very bones of dragons. Dragons, folk heroes, maidens, emperors, and magic all dynamically overlap with one another across folklore.

❖ ❖ ❖

Folk Heroes

Folk heroes take many forms—knights, paupers, and other popular figures beloved by the people they represent. They are often based on a real person in history, a hybrid of several real people, or a common stereotype. They uphold some sort of moral high-ground and often have a litany of adventures attributed to them over the centuries.

Dragons serve two purposes in folk-hero stories: they're either the villain or a kind benefactor that bestows gifts upon the hero for good deeds done.

Maidens

Dragons and maidens have an odd and mildly inconsistent but interesting dynamic! The Italian version of the fairy tale *Beauty and the Beast* actually describes the beast as being something close to a dragon. Dragons are often bewitched by young maidens, dubbing the young, beautiful, and pure of heart as having a *je ne sais quoi* that sings to the beast (sometimes quite literally).

There's another odd connection between maidens and dragons. The Greek word *drakos* was slang for a scoundrel of a man taking advantage of young women. Some stories of dragons' hunger for young women could be allegory for the habits of a certain unsavory type of man.

Kings and Emperors

European rulers are often referred to as dragons. For example, Arthur Pendragon was a draig, the Welsh term for leader of his army. Being the head of the dragon

Sigurd (Norse)

Sigurd slew dragon Fafnir (see page 95) with his sword, "Wrath," and the assistance of Fafnir's still-human brother, Reginn, in the Old Norse epic the *Volsunga Saga* (1275).

implied that the ruler was the brains and the glue keeping his army together.

Additionally, certain Asian countries align dragons and their divinity to royal families. The first emperor of Japan could supposedly trace his lineage back to Ryūjin (see page 109), the Japanese water god of the sea. The Dragon Lord, Lạc Long Quân of Vietnam (see page 93), is part of the creation myth of the Vietnamese people and is said to have sired the first ruler of Vietnam. The Chinese emperors would sit on the Dragon Throne as a symbol of their connection to the divine. The taniwha (see page 136), a draconic water spirit in Māori folklore, were tied to their chiefs.

Dragons are universally considered to be immensely powerful and important to their respective cultures. Rulers aligning themselves to these divine and powerful beasts can encourage the people to think of them as the same.

TRADITIONAL CHINESE MEDICINE

As potent magical creatures, different pieces of dragon anatomy have been used for many remedies over the years. Dragon blood and bones are ingredients used in Traditional Chinese Medicine (TCM). A treatise on TCM provides one of the more in-depth descriptions of the Chinese lóng (see page 130) because, according to the writer, knowing your ingredients leads to better medicine.

Ancient apothecaries would source fossilized bone (dragons' bone) that they would cook and grind into a powder and then turn into a decoction, or alcohol-based tincture. Dragon blood is a red resin derived from the sap of nearly thirty different types of trees. It is used in TCM as an anti-microbial, anti-inflammatory, and pro-collagen treatment. Nowadays, the resin comes in the form of pills.

According to Marco Polo, who observed hunters harvesting a "dragon," the gallbladder of dragons is also used to make a strong and versatile treatment that can cure rabies, ease labor pains and make the baby come faster, and reduce the size of topical growths or swelling. Marco Polo also noted that dragon meat was good to eat and counted as a delicacy.

Seven Dragons in Acupuncture

Acupuncture is a TCM practice that involves inserting fine needles into specific points on the body to alleviate pain, as a form of treatment for certain ailments or as preventative medicine. A classic TCM text describes an old acupuncture practice used to alleviate persistent spiritual ailments, which includes trauma, possession, and certain mental disorders; known as the seven dragons, it would summon spiritual dragons to the body to provide protection for the patient and drive out the possessing spirit.

Taxonomy

Even in the magical and mythological, there are rules. They may not be as stringent as those in astrophysics or molecular biology, but dragons are subject to rules of their own universes, just like the rest of us. In their rules, the age-old adage "magic always has a cost" can be applied to these mystical reptiles. There are different categories of dragons, and they go through life cycles very similar to their raptor cousins . . . not chickens, but rather eagles, falcons, and other birds of prey. This chapter will break dragons down into their pieces and learn about what makes them roar.

TYPES OF DRAGONS

For the purposes of this book, a dragon is physically defined as a large, tailed, reptilian creature from mythology or folklore that can also be described as having any number of additional physical attributes. Some examples of these additional physical attributes are wings, a beard, two or four legs, toes or claws, and/or horns in any number of combinations. Some dragons may be able to fly while others cannot, and the method in which they take flight is subject to change across dragon types.

While some of these subcategories of dragons will seem unique to the dragon as defined above, language in source materials has labeled all these types of creatures as a dragon. Most notably, dragons and wyverns have become interchangeable in most contemporary media. As such, these creatures are all part of dragonkind. If technical correctness matters most in a description of a dragon, the following subcategories are concrete definitions of each type of dragon.

Traditional Dragons

To qualify as a dragon, the creature must have four legs, claws, a scaly hide, a tail, and the ability to fly. They may or may not have wings, depending on the cultural origin of the dragon in question.

Dragons from Asian cultures and folklore typically do not have wings. Their face is a meld between something reptilian and that of a lion. They sometimes have a bushy mane like a lion or a beard like a goat. These dragons have

Snapdragon

This perennial plant goes by the scientific name *Antirrhinum* and sprouts a spike of vibrantly colored flowers. Snapdragons (sometimes called dragon flowers) got their colloquial name because squeezing the flower's sides can open its mouth, which resembles the snapping jaw of a dragon.

serpentine bodies that are usually thick like a tree trunk, and a pair of legs located at the front and the back of their long body. Their tails thin gradually towards the end of their bodies and will often have little tufts of fur or feathers at the very end. While they may prefer traversing through water, as many of them make their homes in rivers and lakes, they can also fly despite their lack of wings.

Dragons in European culture and folklore have four legs, claws, a deadly tail, great bat-like wings that protrude from their shoulder blades, and the muzzle of a giant lizard or snake with numerous sharp teeth in their maw. Their wings are described as bat-like because bones in bat wings replicate that of fingers. One finger-like claw comes out at the crest of the ridges at the top of the wing, and the other three or four 'fingers' spread the skin of the wings taut. Finger-like bones in the wings allow for increased dexterity in flight that adheres to the normal physics associated with the flight of birds and bats.

Wyverns

Wyverns are very similar to dragons from European cultures. They have the same powerful tail, reptilian face, and a pair of wings, but only two legs instead of four. Sometimes, their wings may diverge from dragons, with clawed hands set at the end of their wings. They also may or may not have the bat-like bones that resemble fingers in their wings. While both Asian and European dragons often boast increased mental capabilities and fantasy powers, wyverns are depicted as being more animalistic. They are considered intelligent, their cleverness similar to the way a big cat stalks their prey. Wyverns are rarely portrayed as capable of human speech.

Wyverns are often found in Medieval European heraldry and family crests. During this time, people named any dragon-like creature with four legs and wings as dragons and any dragon-like creatures with two legs and wings as wyverns. In these images, wyverns are usually not portrayed as breathing fire, though this is not true for

48

❖ ❖ ❖

all representations. European dragons and wyverns are often lumped into the same category. The most famous example appears in the fantasy book and television series *Game of Thrones*. Wyverns and dragons both exist in what is called the "Known World" of author George R. R. Martin's creation, but the dragons depicted in the series are technically wyverns by the medieval herald definition. For more on Martin's dragons and wyverns, see page 153.

Serpents and Wyrms

Just like there were general similarities between wyverns and traditional dragons, the long, thick body of the Chinese dragons have a distinctly serpentlike quality to them. Some great mythological serpents of old could fly, much like their dragon counterparts.

The main criteria for dragon-type serpents are that they are big. As in, monstrously huge. In the case of the Dahomey Rainbow Serpent, large enough to be coiled under the earth. These serpents are fearsome but bother with humans much less than other types of dragons.

Much like serpents, wyrms are snakes of unusual size. The word has Germanic roots and is also seen as worms or wurms, depending on the area of origin. Wyrms are distinct from dragons, although the Old Norse word for wyrm is often used in conjunction with dragons. Consider how all snakes are reptiles, but not all reptiles are snakes. Wyrms are a type of serpent and often do not have legs or wings, nor can they fly.

Serpents (and by association, wyrms) show up much more frequently in mythology than any other type of dragon, likely because they are based on a real-life creature that different cultures have actually seen and interacted with rather than an amalgamation of terrifying parts.

Drakes and Dracontopodes

Drakes and dracontopodes bend the rules of what it means to be a dragon. The term drake comes from the Balkan people of Southeastern Europe and usually refers to bipedal (or two-legged) drakes and the quadruped (or four-legged) drakes. The bi-pedal drake is a monstrous dragon-human hybrid that is sometimes represented as a man-eating troll or as a handsome-looking human with the ability to transform into a dragon.

Drakes are fiercely loyal to their family members, and they are one of the more logical types of dragons. Their home is their lair, and one better have a good reason to be there or be invited, lest they want to be devoured. The Ancient Greeks used the term dracontopodes to refer to humanoid dragons.

Conversely, the representation of the four-legged drake is much more animalistic. Sometimes as large as a moose, these drakes are wingless dragons and very similar to monitor lizards or crocodiles. They live in caves and can be aggressive and vicious. While they may not be as intelligent or as mighty as other dragons on this list, they're still formidable foes. However, since their bodies are more of a quadruped than a snake, their tail frequently does not pose the same threat as the tails of other types of dragons.

For the purposes of this book, drakes will refer to wingless draconic quadrupeds, and dracontopodes will refer to dragons that have human forms.

ANATOMY AND BIOLOGY

Key aspects of dragons show up in many of their different representations. Nailing down a specific anatomy of a mythical creature is never easy, especially when many of their defining factors vary across cultures (and sometimes across descriptions of the same dragon). A few things are standard though; for example, dragons are saurian, or an enormous reptile, from which we can infer other clues, such as being cold-blooded like their reptilian counterparts. If a dragon can fly, they may have hollow yet incredibly dense and durable bones like birds.

We may never know the egg of a thought that hatched the idea of dragons. But we can speculate on the inspirations for dragon representations based on the various features of dragon anatomy.

Size

The common denominator across all types of dragons is size. Some are utterly enormous—on the scale of giants in their associated mythos—and others, while still large and formidable, are more in line with the size of megafauna we're used to, such as elephants.

Many of the dragons elevated to divine status were so big that they encircled the earth or rested along the bed of the Nile River. According to Edward Topsell, dragons could grow to about thirty yards long. A famous example of an alleged sighting occurred in 1875, when merchant captain George Drevar claimed that he saw a sea serpent wrapped several times around a whale, wrestling the creature at the surface before dragging it under the waves.

Legs

Legs are an inconsistent feature among dragon depictions. As previously discussed, European heraldry defines a dragon as having four legs and wings and a wyvern as having two legs and wings. Sea serpents and great wyrms do not traditionally have legs, while dragons from Asian cultures are usually more serpentlike but still have short powerful legs. Some sea serpents and aquatic dragons have flippers rather than legs, like the Loch Ness Monster and the mo'o.

Tail

Whether they have wings, legs, claws, or jaws, the tail should be avoided during encounters with the fearsome beast. A dragon tail is described as immensely strong with the ability to constrict and crush air out of their victim's chest. Bishop Isidore of Seville's writing tells an account of a dragon using its tail to trip up creatures as large as an elephant and then suffocating them in this manner.

Modern fictional depictions of dragons also recognize the power of their tail, but frequently add some method of bludgeoning or slashing to the tip to convey its deadliness.

Dragon Hide and Scales

Dragon scales are often described as being near-impenetrable. Dragons in China and Japan were said to sometimes transform into pine trees, leaving their scales bark-like. In the Old Testament, the Leviathan's hide is described as having scales so tightly tucked together that not even air can pass through, and iron cannot pierce them. Iron is one of the few elements that can potentially penetrate a dragon's scales, as seen in Greek mythology when Cadmus slew Ares's guardian.

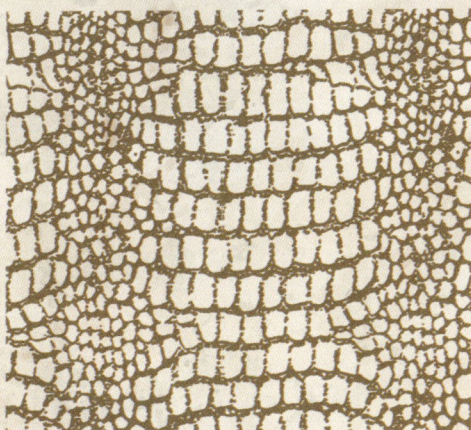

While dragons are reptiles, and reptiles routinely shed their skin, there are few-to-no tales of finding shed dragon skin. One interesting account is that of a Christian monk sending a 120-foot-long (37 m) snakeskin, that was nearly as wide as it was long, to the senate of the Byzantine Empire.

Claws or Talons

Some dragons have reptilian claws, while others have bird-like talons. Some interpretations even bestow dragons with powerful feline paws and claws. The number of toes also differs across descriptions, although three or four were most common.

Asian dragons, while quite similar, are often differentiated by their number of toes: Japanese dragons have three, Korean dragons have four or five, and Chinese dragons have five. There are cultural explanations for the differing number of toes. According to the Japanese perspective, they believe that their tatsu or ryu (see page 137) liked to travel. As it did, it would gain toes for each new person they encountered.

Skull

The skull of a dragon was home to many magical and powerful artifacts. According to Bishop Isidore of Seville, there was a treasured gem, draconite, within the skull of dragons. It could only be harvested from a live dragon; if removed from a dead dragon, the gem would lose its luster. Chinese lóngs are often described as having a pearl tucked under their chin that they'd gift to folk heroes who did them a great favor. These pearls granted luck and prosperity.

Supposedly, dragon teeth were also highly magical. In ancient Greece, the goddess Athena told the founder of Thebes, Cadmus, to plant the teeth from a dragon he'd slain. When he did so, soldiers sprung up from them like flowers and turned the battle in Cadmus's favor.

Different dragons have different snouts—either squashed like a bulldog, tusked like an elephant, long and small like an anteater, or like the powerful and toothy jaws of alligators. Each of these muzzles tell a lot about the temperament and disposition of the dragon. For example, smaller snouted dragons in Macedonia were little more than domesticated house cats. Women would raise them as part of their family alongside their children, some stories going as far to say that they would demand to be fed from the same breast as the human child. Alternatively, a twelfth-century French poet remarked that dragons with mouths as large as a cauldron would attempt to take down predators like lions.

Horns

Some dragons have horns or antlers, depending on the area that they're from. This may blend the imagery of the horns of devils or demons, or they could be calling on the biology of fossilized creatures. Horns can mean different things across cultures.

When thinking of the horned serpent of Native American mythology, horns seem to be a key indicator that this creature is no regular serpent. Antlers are part of the general description of Chinese lóng. Juvenile Korean dragons, imugi, must complete tasks or live to a certain age before they grow their horns as adult yeongs.

Plumes, Feathers, and Crests

Quetzalcoatl is known across Mayan or Aztec mythology as being a feathered or plumed serpent. Many dragons, Asian ones in particular, have decorative crests on their heads. Crests are made from something like feathers and horns, so one can assume that they're made of keratin (or the same sturdy and durable material that makes up hair, nails, horns, feathers, beaks, shells, and scales).

If the idea of dragons derives from dinosaur fossils, it is possible that ancient archaeologists found fossilized or preserved remains and assumed these prehistoric monsters were feathered. Plumes, feathers, and crests usually adorn dragons in a manner that looks like a crown. In medieval bestiaries, crowned dragons would be exceedingly prideful.

Life Cycle of a Dragon

Egg: Which came first, the dragon or the egg? Dragon eggs are usually rare, which means that dragons are very protective of their broods. They can be laid by dragons or created through a magical ritual, as is the case with the basilisk, which hatches from a chicken egg.

Hatchling: Hatchlings are about the size of a housecat. There are a few myths of humans finding and tending to hatchlings, including one from the Middle Ages about a boy and a hatchling growing up together.

Wyrmling: The bosha is an example of a wyrmling, where a dragon begins as something before evolving into a fully formed dragon while surviving independently of their parents quite young.

Mature Adult: According to Traditional Chinese Medicine, dragons mate as the male spirals on a downdraft while the female spirals on an updraft. Some of these stories also indicate that dragons may turn into regular snakes after they mate, which would make dragon young quite prized.

Ancient Elder: A wise dragon can live for potentially more than a thousand years. These dragons are far from feeble. Older dragons are usually considered the most fearsome.

Blood

In Traditional Chinese Medicine (TCM), dragon blood has a variety of uses and comes from a variety of sources. Some ancient people would use elephant blood as dragon blood, while others referred to the sap of a dracaena tree, which runs dark red and viscous.

In European dragon lore, dragon's blood often had the caustic and melting effects of acid on all living creatures. Many dragons would use the toxicity of their blood to ensure their slayer also perished.

ABILITIES

Dragons boast a host of abilities across the many myths they appear in. Below are some of the most common draconic abilities that appear in their depictions.

Flight

Not all dragons can fly, but those that can are agile and talented fliers. Their preferred method of transportation seems equally split between the ground and the sky. Some dragons fly with large leathery bat wings. The more serpentine dragons are also sometimes capable of flight, like Chinese lóngs. Korean yeongs have a special node in their head that grants them the ability to levitate. Some Rainbow Serpents in Native Australian Dreamtime mythology can fly through the sky as a rainbow to hop from different bodies of water.

❖ ❖ ❖

Strength

Strength and durability are essential dragon attributes. For example, Leviathan can cut through copper and iron with its claws, teeth, and tail. In the previously mentioned Drevar sighting, the strong coils of a sea serpent had enough might to strangle a whale. The *Etymologies'* definition of a dragon cites the dragon's ability to trip up enormous creatures like elephants by wrapping their body around its legs. Snakes are essentially one long chord of muscle, and dragons boast proportional strength to their serpentine counterparts.

Heightened Senses

Keen sight, smell, and hearing are all abilities that dragons boast. It might be why the bashful guivre in France (see page 128) averts its eyes to nudity—it sees something the rest of us cannot.

Winckelreidt (Switzerland)

Winckelreidt was a murderer who was offered the chance of redemption if he slayed the dragon of Dewilder/Wilser. Winckelreidt was victorious for only a brief moment after he delivered a killing blow to the beast. The dragon, knowing it would be the last thing it did, threw itself upon its slayer, pinning him to the ground with its mass, while its caustic blood drained from its body and poisoned Winckelreidt to death.

Their hyper-awareness not only makes them fearsome predators but also difficult to trick or take advantage of. The dragon from *Beowulf* (see page 144) knew when a single chalice of his was taken, and he followed the thief's scent all the way home.

Their hearing is renowned—a useful ability as dragons can be fiercely loyal to those who befriend them. According to legends, if ever you call for assistance after doing a dragon a favor, they will swiftly fly to your aid. Distance rarely matters. Dragons will travel miles to rescue those they are fond of.

Shapeshifting

Shapeshifting dragons can change their size, transform into other creatures, or even take on a humanoid form. Chinese dragons are sometimes linked to giants, who look like large humans. Also in Chinese mythology, Dragon Kings and their families will present themselves as human.

In several myths, dragons transform into humans to interact with local populations. They will often do so to seduce young and beautiful women. In one particular myth, a dragon would annually come to collect the most beautiful and brave woman from town. If the young maiden was brave and pure of heart, the dragon would bless her with gifts. If she flinched in the dragon's presence, he'd eat her whole.

Speed

Whether by water or by air, dragons are a force to be reckoned with when it comes to speed. In 1876, while aboard the *S. S. Nestor*, John W. Webster made note of a large black dragon (crew estimated about two hundred feet, or 61 m, long) with a square head keeping pace with their boat. This far outpaces the fastest recorded aquatic sea creature, the black marlin, which can swim at about eighty-two miles per hour (132 km/h).

Breath

Many dragons have a special breath ability tied to whatever lore has inspired it. Whether it's fire, poison, lightning, clouds, or other noxious fumes, many people do not think a dragon is a dragon without their ability to exhale death onto their prey. This may be related to the venom found in many snake bites, or to pollution, or to the dragon's link to water. The Grimm Bothers, Jacob and Wilhelm, heavily influenced our definition of dragons as having some sort of deadly breath, particularly the fiery one we associate with dragons today.

- **Venom and Poison:** Poison is a more prevalent trait to dragons than both flight and the ability to breathe fire. Along with being horrible to behold, dragons were not only poisonous by their bite, but their presence could be a blight on the local plant life. In the Early Modern Era, it was believed dragons reached this level of high toxicity by eating poisonous plants in the wilderness they called home.

  Dragons are widely known for their toxicity. Some possess breath so caustic that they vaporize any living creature caught in the belched toxins. A single blow from a dragon can fell their slayer (as was the case for Beowulf), though epic poetry and modern interpretations sometimes view this as a single venomous bite.

Their mouths are sometimes described as dripping venom. In cases where dragons were aligned with the devil, this venom was often a metaphor for lies dripping from demons' mouths that could kill or damn a person, all the same.

⊛ **Smoke and Smog:** Certain accounts of dragons existing in toxic clouds are likely linked to pollution. The use of coal in Europe began in the Middle Ages (as early as the eleventh and twelfth centuries), and toxic pollution and "bad air" is a known by-product of coal power and heating. Several centuries later came the large smog clouds we associate with the Industrial Revolution.

Dragons breathing noxious, choking fumes is likely linked to the extent of pollution from that burning coal. Coal burning caused a new phenomenon, and dragons offered a reason for something people didn't

Dragonstone Crystal

A dragonstone crystal is characterized by a ruddy red brick color with thick mossy veins running throughout. It is said to unlock the heart and magnify energies. Many people meditate with it to help manifest goals or move through difficult emotions, particularly grief. This stone could be linked to the draconite stone found in the heads of living dragons.

understand. In fact, we only scientifically understood the consequences burning coal had on the lungs in the early 1900s, one hundred years after coal's introduction.

Clouds and Rain: Across the globe, dragons are linked to water and strongly tied to storms. Some iterations cite them as fearing thunder, likely because of the numerous ancient myths featuring dragons being bested by storm gods. Other explanations suggest that dragons were particularly dry creatures who would immolate when struck by lightning.

Despite the Western dragons' aversion to thunder and lightning, Asian dragons can breathe out clouds and make rain. These clouds could be light and fluffy across a blue sky or the type that produce heavy rainstorms, and in some cases (when the dragon feels slighted or upset) great floods. In these myths, the types of clouds created are often indicative of the dragon's mood.

Fire: The scorching fire that dragons rained down on villages during their raids was a terrifying prospect. In modern dragon stories, dragon fire burns hotter than normal fire and forging items in dragon flame can sometimes bestow that object with magical properties—an excellent quality for fantasy weapons and armor.

While dragons are magical, keeping fire in one's stomach is an impossibility for living creatures. One explanation for a dragon's ability to belch flames is that they are actually exhaling some sort of poisonous, flammable gas ignited by a spark from one of their teeth.

WEAKNESSES

Even the strongest soldiers will have a vulnerable joint in their armor. Dragons are no different. Myths and legends of dragonkind are filled with objects and methods to defeat these beasts.

- **Holy Symbols:** In Medieval European tales, dragons were weakened by holy symbols, such as making the sign of the cross. Holy water was also an effective way to neutralize a dragon, as seen with Tarasque (see page 112).

- **Softer Insides:** Although no one ever wants to get devoured by a dragon, cutting oneself out from the inside can be an effective way to find freedom and surpass the toughness of a dragon's hide. For example, the Dragon of Wantley in South Yorkshire, England, was famously ravenous and would eat literally everything in its path. A brave knight, known as Sir Moore, cleverly commissioned a spiked suit of armor, and when he was swallowed, he kicked the dragon's gut with his spiked boot, causing the creature to perish.

- **Iron or Gold:** Medieval European dragons were often defeated by gallant knights wielding iron swords. Lóngs in China, especially the Dragon Kings (see page 126), were also weak to swords, and there were two powerful dragons who were felled by a gold armlet.

- **Neck:** Many dragons met their demise via beheading or being sliced in two. Ketil Trout, a Norse chieftain, is said to have bisected a dragon with his trusty axe.

❖ ❖ ❖

- ⚙ **Music:** Music soothes the savage beast, and while that's true for some dragons, others find it a downright awful sound. In some tales, singing or playing music was the best chance at escaping a menacing aspis, a European wyvern deathly poisonous to touch, which will plug up one ear with its tail and smash its other ear to the ground to block out a tune.

- ⚙ **Frankincense:** Edward Topsell indicated that dragons in Egypt and Saudi Arabia could not stand the smell of frankincense, and that the Boswellia tree from which it comes prevented those areas from being overrun with dragons.

- ⚙ **Peridexion Tree:** Medieval bestiaries state that in their native habitat of India, the fruit and shadow of the Peridexion Tree (which are loved and inhabited by doves) can kill a dragon. This could be a metaphor to stay close to the path of goodness and righteousness, lest evil eat you up.

❖ ❖ ❖

- **Hayseed Dust:** Peppering oneself with hayseed dust could keep dragons from biting. This worked better with the Macedonian domesticated dragons that were nursed by human mothers and that played with and slept alongside human children.

- **Girdles:** In the Middle Ages, a girdle was a type of clothing worn by both men and women. This pre-corset cinched formless and flowing fabrics at the waist. There are several tales in which a gallant knight weakens the beast so that a girl may put her girdle over its snout and lead the docile creature around. An example of this is seen in the tale of Martha and Saint George, where George uses a sword to distract and weaken an Ethiopian dragon, giving Martha the time to muzzle the beast with her girdle.

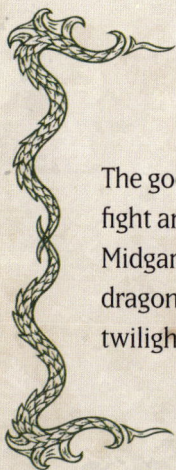

Thor (Norse)

The god of thunder in Nordic mythology loves a good fight and longed to do battle against the gigantic Midgard serpent since the beast's inception. Both dragon and god slay each other during Ragnarök, the twilight of the gods in Norse myths.

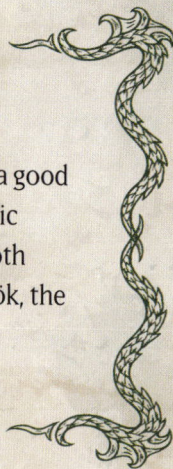

- **Strong Liquor:** Dragons have a weakness for the pleasures of life. While they're enormous and powerful, they are not immune to hangovers and inebriation. A 1923 newspaper reported on the death of a snallygaster (see page 135) that was lured to a distillery and drowned after falling into a huge vat of moonshine.

- **Sleeping Medicines:** In *Etymologies*, there's a story of a brave group of villagers leaving grains laced with a sleeping tonic close to a dragon's lair. The dragon greedily gobbled up the grains and fell into a deep sleep, which allowed the villagers to cut the dragonstone from its head.

- **Catching Them Mid Feast:** In the *Saga of Thidreks of Bern*, an old Norse saga from sometime around 1250, Prince Dietrich and his companion Fasold come upon a dragon attempting to devour whole a man named Sistram. Sistram knows that the dragon cannot eat and fight at the same time. Thus the huge, flying dragon with its long snout, thick legs, and ironlike claws, is unable to defend itself as Sistram remains partially devoured in its mouth.

- **Bonfire Smoke:** Bonfires were originally called "bone fires." In Europe during the Middle Ages, the smoke from great pyres of burnt bone could be used to ward an area against dragons for miles. According to John Beleth, a twelfth-century French theologian, this was done to defend against dragons that would ejaculate into water sources and poison the people who lived there.

❖ ❖ ❖

DIET

Many myths depict dragons enjoying all manner of livestock, either by the dragon stealing them or taxing the communities of surrounding areas with a livestock tithe to satisfy their hunger. According to myths, locals consented to this practice as no one wants a hungry dragon in their backyard. These tithes also frequently included one human a year, chosen by lottery.

Edward Topsell dove deeply into their nature in his writings. He stated that dragons can live for a long time without food but become increasingly ravenous and unpredictable the longer they go without eating. Some dragons were said to heal themselves by eating fennel. Others would eat plants to regurgitate anything unsettling their stomachs. Topsell also notes that dragons grow in size by eating their own kind.

Not all dragons are meat eaters. For example, the Lithuanian Aitvaras, a household dragon that would bring luck and good fortune in exchange for the residents' souls, was quite fond of omelets. In Homer's epic poem *The Iliad*, he notes that they'd also eat poisonous plants to help increase their toxicity.

According to Marco Polo's account of seeing dragons along his travels, dragons would eat lion and bear cubs. *Etymologies's* description of a dragon taking down an elephant suggests that elephants may be on the menu. One myth about Chinese Dragon Kings notes a particular taste for swallows, and that gifting them hundreds or thousands of the birds could endear them to the giver and initiate a gift-giving exchange.

❖ ❖ ❖

TREASURE

Some dragons sit upon a mountain of treasure, but it was commonly believed that certain dragons could make treasure. During the fourth century CE, it was believed that a dragon resided in the treasury of Constantinople, what is now modern-day Istanbul, Turkey. Chinese lóngs had a "dragon pearl" under their chin that could grant its owner immense luck and prosperity, which they would gift to people who did them a favor.

In Europe, tales from the Roman author, Pliny the Elder, inspired the belief that dragons had a dragonstone within their skull. This could only be retrieved from living or recently deceased dragons. Likewise, the ancient Greek philosopher Plato tells a story of the Ring of Gyges (a treasure that grants the wearer invisibility) being hidden behind a dragon's eye.

Japanese Dragon Kings, in particular, bestow interesting gifts. In the *Tale of Tawaratopa*, the hero Hidesato helps a Dragon King slay its mortal enemy, the centipede. The gifts he receives as payment are a ream of never-ending silk, a cookpot that makes everything delicious, and a bag of rice that never empties.

ANIMAL RIVALRIES

When dragons are considered part of the animal world, they are also attributed a position in the food chain. A rivalry with other creatures in the natural world emerged. Due to medieval literature's tendency to describe dragon habitats as being far away from Europe, the animal was often non-native to the continent.

- **Elephant:** The elephant is the most prolific of the animal rivalries. This likely comes from Pliny the Elder's work, *Natural Histories*, where dragons lurk in brush to trip up elephants.

- **Panther:** According to many a medieval bestiary, dragons fear their roar so much that they'll retreat to their lair or a cave to hide from the big cat. This may be because panther dander and odor can lock up a dragon's joints and petrify them.

- **Dove:** Doves roost in the Peridexion tree and as such, dragons hate them. Whether that be because they carry something in their talons from the bark of the tree or savor its sweet fruit remains unclear.

Centipede: According to Chinese mythology, lóngs are natural enemies to giant centipedes, with one Dragon King requesting assistance from a human to defeat his rival.

Eagle: Both raptors of the air, eagle and dragons have a contentious relationship, according to Edward Topsell. The pair are said to try and snatch away each other's meals from their talons. Eagles have also been known to smash the eggs of dragons, which would explain why the flapping of an eagle's wings and the rustling of their feathers can spook dragons into flying straight home to protect their unhatched clutch.

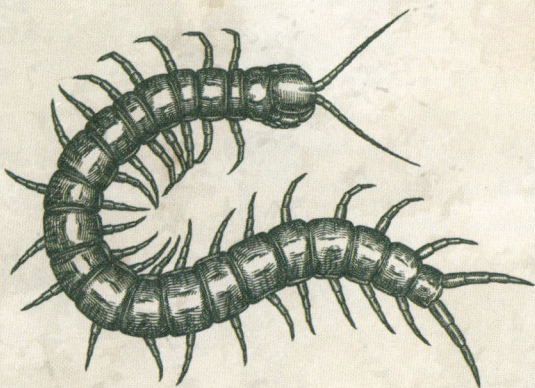

Dragon-Related Symbolism

A dragon is never just a dragon. They can represent the might of a nation or the faith of an entire people nestled on the shoulders of a ruler or general. The hope they symbolize can sour and transform a dragon into a tyrant just begging to be deposed. Dragons can also be typecast as a villain, the embodiment of wanton greed and senseless destruction. When they spin in a circle, an ouroboros eating its tail, they're in tune with nature and the cycles that come with it. They're gracious water spirits, divine guides, and our innermost demons all at once.

❖ ❖ ❖

WHAT DRAGONS REPRESENT

Dragons can mean a lot of things in myths and modern media. Even at their inception, they were often considered metaphors for large concepts rather than something people staunchly believed in. Vritra, for example, is both a metaphor for drought and a well-known deity in India. Across the many myths and legends of dragonkind, there are common threads of symbolism.

Resources and Greed

The hoard of a dragon may appear as shining gold and jewels, but their fortune is a metaphor for more than something shiny. In Old Norse Mythology, dragons that hoarded resources eroded the social cohesion of the group. Any build-up of gold in one place signified an unequal distribution of resources. When equal distribution was not carried out, the people's faith in their leadership deteriorated. Without the support and trust of their people, the chiefs were mere steps away from being deposed.

You can see this idea at play in *Beowulf*, in which the dragon's treasure is cursed and burned rather than used. The curse isn't in the treasure itself, but rather the greed that led to its gathering.

Likewise, an insurrection in Laon, France, in 1112 was later described as being the work of a five-headed dragon that rained down fire from its flight. One miserly deacon tried to save his belongings by setting them on a boat and nudging them into the river rather than helping his community. The dragon took a break from his destruction of the town to specifically torch the deacon's belongings. Later, this was interpreted as punishment for the deacon's greed in a time of crisis.

Power

Imposing physical prowess, aligned with kings and emperors, and sitting atop a mound of gold—there is no doubt that dragons have literal and metaphorical power. Whether that be political, physical, or monetary, dragons' possession of this power is not always a bad thing.

Many of the Asian myths that portray dragons in a positive light show that dragons take their responsibility to the regions they rule over seriously. Beloved by their people as capricious problem-solvers, the dragons in these myths exercise their power in the name of benevolence and the greater good as much as they do on a whim.

Indra (India)

The storm god did battle with the fearsome serpent Vritra (see page 116), who had consumed all the water in the world. Indra drank an energizing beverage and flew into a rage that allowed him to kill Vritra with a lightning bolt.

Insurmountable Odds

Dragons are frequently the "final boss," or the ultimate creature to beat in video games, stories, and epic fantasy sagas. Strong and backed up by numerous abilities, they are almost always the Goliath to be unseated by an unlikely underdog. They symbolize the impossible, both in the sense that they're fantastical and that any hope of besting a dragon is slim to none. The flip side to this gilded coin is that when insurmountable odds are presented in a myth, they're almost always set up to frame what seems impossible as possible.

SLAYING A DRAGON

Myths often portray slaying a dragon as a test of strength or honor, as well as cleverness. While there is a plethora of methods throughout dragon-slaying myths, the common denominator in most of these instances is that they require more than just brute strength to ensure the slayer's victory.

- **Traps:** Marco Polo indicated that dragon hunters did not engage the beasts to slay them directly. Instead, low on the ground along known dragon paths, the hunters would set up hidden razors on spikes that could grievously wound the creature as it made its way to a watering hole. Dragons being fearsome creatures even when wounded, hunters would wait until they heard carrion birds cawing at the water, which indicated the creature was slain and the coast was clear.

- **Tricks:** Manipulating a dragon's ferocious appetite and getting them to ingest something that will either make them sleep or otherwise incapacitate them makes slaying the fearful creature that much easier.

- ⚜ **Beheading:** A common method of slaying any monstrous creature is beheading, if one has the strength to lob off its monstrous head and the guts to get close enough to do so.

- ⚜ **Hubris:** Manipulating a dragon's hubris inevitably gives the slayer the upper hand. This is evident in Greek mythology with the sky god Zeus's defeat of the draconic titan, Typhon. Typhon lifts a mountain to throw at an incapacitated Zeus—a truly impressive feat!—but it backfires when Zeus hurls a lightning bolt at Typhon, and the dragon drops the mountain on its head, burying itself alive.

TAMING A DRAGON

Some stories of dragons, especially those after the Middle Ages, focused on the ability to train dragons. These tales indicate a shift in attitudes toward dragons and different ideas of showcasing strength and intelligence through taming these imposing creatures rather than killing them. The normally fearsome beasts could have their temperament manipulated by certain acts of care, and in some myths, dragons are portrayed as faithful creatures that could make good pets.

- **Finding the Correct Dragon:** While every dragon has the capacity to be swayed by kindness, there are some breeds of dragons that are predisposed to friendliness with humans. The mark of a domesticated dragon is in their snout. The thinner snouts (which are good for fishing but not so good for devouring humans whole) are more easily tamed. One particular breed in Macedonian myths would grow to the size of a house cat or dog, and they would sometimes, if well-fed, nurse the other animals.

- **Bravery:** Dragons admire bravery, and if you show that you're fearless even when the odds are stacked against you, they'll be more inclined to not only leave you undevoured but also stay at your side.

- **Uncommon Kindness:** The way many peasants and simple folk won the heart of a dragon was to just be immensely good. A Japanese fairy tale tells the story of a fisherman who saw some children tormenting a turtle and turning it on its back. He immediately stopped them and set the turtle free. The turtle turned out to be the daughter of the Dragon King. The Dragon Princess brought the fisherman to her father's house and showed him the wonders of the palace. Eventually the two fell in love and were wed.

Bountiful Gifts: There are many tales where dragons demand sacrifices of meat, men, or maiden, but when a gift is freely given, the creature is easily won over. The amount of food a dragon requires is immense, and they can also be swayed by gold and other finery.

Feeding by Hand: When a newborn dragon is found, or simply a young dragon for that matter, feeding it by hand is an excellent way to acclimate it to human kindness.

Raising Hatchling: One story of a dragon from the 1600s described a young lord who kept a dragon in his bed. The two were raised in tandem, as if the dragon were just as human as the child. One day, his parents grew wary of the dragon's size. They placed the bed that the child and dragon slept in outside while both were sleeping, and while the boy found his way home, the dragon absconded to the woods to begin his life as a wild creature. One day when the boy, now a young man, was beset upon by bandits in the woods, he called out in pain, and his saurian childhood playmate heard and rushed to the scene to eviscerate the highwaymen assaulting him.

- ❁ **Consistency:** A dragon's love is hard won and not easily walked away from. There are several stories of young maidens that would keep dragons in their rooms or receive regular visits from a dragon, but when the maiden was spirited away (or perhaps she left intentionally), the dragon, when it found her again, became irritable and spiteful and would bite or whip the woman with its tail.

DRAGONS AS GODS

Early cultures have no shortage of dragon-like gods and monstrous serpents. These dragon gods are often represented as larger-than-life forces of nature intrinsic to the creation of the world.

Dragonslayer Storm Gods

A pattern often seen in early myths is enmity between dragons and gods associated with weather and storms. For example, in Babylonian mythology, the chief god Marduk throws a storm

in the dragon Tiâmat's mouth and uses her incapacitation to rip her in two, creating the sky and oceans from her larger-than-life remains. In the Indian myth of the battle between the dragon, Vritra, and the storm god, Indra, Vritra is the personification of drought. Through epic battle, the god of storm releases the water from the vile serpent's body.

In Greek mythology, the sky and storm god, Zeus, battles the reptilian titan and father of monsters, Typhon. According to myth, the creation of Typhon was a last-ditch effort by the earth titan, Gaia, to punish Zeus for overthrowing the titans and being crowned king of the Greek pantheon. Typhon symbolizes the chaotic wilderness, and Zeus symbolizes society and order.

These clashes are analogies meant to teach their audiences, like many myths do. In several of these tales, the dragons hoard rain inside their bodies, and the storm gods tear the dragons apart to release the rain and allow the people to flourish.

Keepers of the Underworld

The underworld can seem dark and dastardly, and dragons lurking in its depths are almost always demonized. Various myths have dragons that occupy the underworld: the Egyptian serpent god of chaos and night, Apep, who attempts to metaphorically eat the sun every time it passes into his realm; the Norse Nidhogg, who lives in Hel and gnaws on the roots of the Tree of Life as well as on the souls of malicious humans; in Christianity, Satan is said to take the form of a dragon and live in a version of the underworld;

in Greek mythology, a giant serpent slithers through the river of the dead, Styx, to soundproof the world of the living against the screams of the deceased; and in Iroquois mythology, the Great Horned Serpent resides in the great below and world of the spirits.

Cosmic Serpent

Cosmic, or Rainbow, Serpents are common dragons in early mythology. They exist at the beginning of the universe, and all life on Earth starts with their divine will. Aido Hwedo, the Rainbow Serpent of the Dahomey People of West Africa, rode through the primordial sea and shaped the earth with its enormous body. When the call came, it took up the mantle to prop up the Earth and keep it from falling into the abyss.

Tiâmat, the evil and vengeful serpent from Babylonian mythology, is also the creator of all the other gods. Nuwa, a half-snake–half-human goddess from Chinese creation myths, is responsible for not only creating all human life, but reestablishing the pillars of the earth that hold the heavens in the sky.

EASTERN VIEW: POWER AND NATURAL BALANCE

Eastern dragons, specifically those of China, Japan, and Korea, are an imperial symbol, something that holds society together and provides protection. These creatures are in tune with the universe and seek to keep the delicate balance intact. Many of these creatures are larger

❖ ❖ ❖

than life and hold immense power, a responsibility they shoulder nobly, for the most part.

Harmony and Balance

Eastern dragons traditionally promote harmony and synergy between people and the land. They're connected to nature and the cycle of life and death. Chinese lóngs, keepers of rain, will hibernate in the winter when rain is sparse.

The Rainbow Serpent of Australian Dreamtime mythology will also hibernate in the mud during the time when it is not the rainy season. These dragons have strong connections to the natural world, and many people caution against imposing on the dragons' territory. Even the masculine yang energy of Chinese dragons call for an equal and opposite ying energy in the phoenix. These dragons cut chaos with order and hold the world around them to that standard.

Here There Be Dragons

It's a common misconception that medieval map makers would warn of dragons in areas unknown and not on their maps. The Latin phrase *Hic sunt dracones* does show up on a globe or two, but it is much less ubiquitous than we think. Colloquially, it means that something is unknown and therefore dangerous.

❖ ❖ ❖

Spirits of Water

Most, if not all, draconic figures in Eastern mythology are linked to water. Whether they be streams or rivers or the iridescent sheen of a rainbow in the air, dragons are creatures of great majesty and beauty. Dragons and Dragon Kings had the ability to gift rain during a drought or curse the ungrateful with an unrelenting monsoon. The people of China and Japan would pray to their dragons (lóng and ryu) for rain and be grateful for every drop. Lạc Long Quân of Vietnam is the patriarch of the Vietnamese people and a proclaimed creature of the water.

Eastern dragons' link to water has a healthy sense of both awe and fear. While water is life-giving, it can also cause devastating floods. Dragons as water spirits don't demand

St. George (Ethiopia/Libya)

There are a few tales of St. George's head-to-head with a dragon. While the location may change, the dragon in question was almost always devouring at least two sheep a day until a lottery for human sacrifices was held. St. George comes upon the King's daughter, who is bravely awaiting her devourment, and he insists on helping her. Together, they best the beast and use her girdle to lead the now-docile dragon to her people, who seek their revenge by killing the beast.

respect, but the people that venerate them see their full potential for love and wrath. This ties into the other belief of balance and synergy.

WESTERN VIEW: GREAT EVIL

Western dragons are usually antisocial monsters that are ferocious and filled with bloodlust. Some of the more intelligent ones enjoy tormenting humans. They are also a symbol of the unknown wild. All of the European medieval bestiaries describe the homes and origins of dragons as being either far-flung (Ethiopia, Africa, India, the Middle East) or in isolated locations in the wilderness.

Devil and Demons

As Christianity co-opted dragons and water spirits and labeled them malevolent demons rather than nature spirits, a shift began to take place. The fire they breathed was hellfire, and dragons were often portrayed as either trying to tempt saints away from their faith or as obstacles that goodly saints were meant to tame and slay.

The popularity of dragons in literature in the Middle Ages is partially due to this perspective. Dragons became a representation of *all* pagan deities and spirits and were labeled as nefarious and sinful creatures.

Ill Omens

In the Middle Ages in Europe, monasteries would have chroniclers for their areas. These records are beneficial for later historians gathering information on their localities.

Dragon Symbols

Ouroboros: Originally a Greek symbol of a serpent eating its tail. It represents the cycle of life, death, and rebirth in an everlasting circle.

Dragon's Eye: A triangle with a "Y" connecting all three points is considered a dragon's eye symbol. Germanic and/or Nordic in origins, it can either mean the balance among love, power, and wisdom, or the crossroads of decision.

Infinity Sign: While not exclusively dragon related, the Egyptian deities were depicted coiled in descending figure-eight-like imagery to show their unfathomable size. This ethos is replicated in the infinity sign for mathematics, which was created by English mathematician John Wallis in 1655.

Heraldry: European heraldry in the Middle Ages was a way to announce armies and people and was a source of pride for the houses that each heraldic symbol represented. Dragons, wyverns, and other mythical creatures were frequently used to symbolize power and strength.

Dragon Pearl: A symbol of great luck and prosperity, dragon pearls were common in Eastern dragons (particularly the Chinese and Korean dragons). Dragons kept this pearl under their chin and would give it to good souls who did them a favor or showed kindness to them or their kin.

At the time of their writing, dragons were used as omens for what was in store in the area. Rodolfus Glaber was a French monk chronicling the area of Auxerre, France when he recorded a dragon sighting on Christmas Eve in 997 CE. Later, this would be labeled as an omen for the civil war that broke out in Burgundy, France.

It wasn't just European monks that saw ill will in dragons. As stated on page 31, a young Merlin was able to divine the fate of the Britons by the outcome of a battle between a white dragon and red dragon.

DRAGONS AS TYRANTS

Consider the profile of a dragon: physical might, a mound of cursed riches at their feet collected from charred corpses, and so high above a common man that they literally fly. Many cultures, in fact, incorporate some form of the word "dragon" into their leaders' titles. The wanton violence and general depiction as being a malicious beast certainly explains the inclination to link these creatures to iron-fisted rulers. Consider Vlad the Impaler (1431–1476), the tyrannical prince of Wallachia known by the nickname Dracula. Although Dracula is now widely recognized to be a vampire thanks to Bram Stoker's epistolary novel, Dracula literally means "son of Dracul," and "Dracul" translates to dragon. This technically means that Dracula's father was the dragon and that Dracula could be . . . well, just about any type of monster, it would seem.

Many European myths depict dragons as villains, and we can see that ideology reproduced in much of fantasy media (see page 146).

Legendary Dragons

Behold the dragons of myth—deities, cautionary tales, life-giving spirits of nature, and fearsome monsters guarding their hoards. These famous beasts of old have lived many lives, first in the folklore and mythology from which they emerged, and later in modern-day media that seeks to pay homage to legendary creatures from the past. For centuries, dragons have captured the attention of the people who believe in them. Either one of a kind or the king among the riot, these dragons boast unique abilities and are key characters in the stories in which they appear.

AIDO HWEDO / AYIDA-WEDDO

Culture of Origin: Dahomey Peoples (modern-day West Africa)
Type: Serpent
Habitat: The depths of the ocean and the cosmic sea
Lore: A male or female serpent of the Dahomey Peoples and commonly referred to as a Rainbow Serpent, Aido Hwedo has a red head and a blue tail and is too immense for one person to see.

At the beginning of time, the moon goddess of creation, Mawu, rode through the universe astride Aido Hwedo's gargantuan body. When they settled on Earth, Aido Hwedo would feast on iron ore found in the ground, and after it was consumed, his waste would make mountain ranges. As Aido Hwedo became too large, he coiled around himself over seven thousand times to hold up the earth in the primordial sea. He's crushed under the weight and will sometimes writhe in pain, which causes earthquakes. Under the earth's crust, he continues to devour iron until there's none left. Once the iron runs out, he'll feast on his own tail. Once he consumes himself entirely, there will be nothing left to hold up the rest of the world, and the earth will fall into the primordial ocean.

Aido Hwedo has also traveled—the Haitian Ayida is their cosmic Voudou counterpart. Ayida is also female in Dahomey and Fon mythologies, and her partner, another cosmic serpent called Damballah, lives on the sun. Whenever he reaches out to her, his fiery body causes canyons to dip into the earth's crust.

AMARU

Culture of Origin: Incan and Andean (modern-day Peru)
Type: Wyvern/Serpent
Habitat: Underworld
Lore: Yet another Rainbow Serpent, Amaru lurks beneath the surface of the world in Ukhu Pacha, the inner earth (or underworld) in Incan mythology. When speaking of Amaru, it could either be the name of the serpent god or a type of two-headed wyvern that is a much lesser dragon sent on malicious errands. When an Amaru dies, it turns to stone.

Like Aido Hwedo (see page 90), Amaru is so vast that when he moves, it causes mountains to move. Like many cosmic serpents, he is connected to water sources.

APEP

Culture of Origin: Ancient Egyptian
Type: Serpent
Habitat: Deep in the Nile and in the Underworld
Lore: In the beginning, there was a yawning void, and from it came the roaring moon serpent, Apep, the god of chaos, darkness, and destruction. Descriptions of this deity range from a giant serpent with a human face, to something closer to a crocodile, or a truly enormous reptile. Apep is malicious, possessing a hunger that was as infamous as it was boundless.

Every night, the sun god Ra made his way through the underworld that Apep called home, and every night, the serpent would unhinge its jaw to swallow him whole in an attempt to keep the sun from the mortal world. Celestial events such as an eclipse were signs that Apep's strength was nearly too great for Ra to best. If the serpent ever succeeded in eating the sun god, Ra would cut himself from Apep's stomach as a symbol of light triumphing over chaos and darkness. But chaos (and Apep) would rarely stay defeated for long.

When not trying to consume his mortal enemy, Apep also devoured the souls of mortals on their way to their final resting place. One depiction shows Apep growing up to twelve heads, a new one sprouting for every soul consumed. If those consumed weren't freed by Apep's destruction, they would have suffered a fate worse than no afterlife—complete obliteration from the universe, utter nonexistence.

Apep is frequently pictured as a long serpent looping coils around itself. Other times, it's pictured in pieces, as when Ra

❖ ❖ ❖

escapes from Apep's body. There is another depiction of Ra as a cat chopping Apep into dismembered pieces.

DRAGON LORD, LẠC LONG QUÂN

Culture of Origin: Vietnamese
Type: Dragon
Habitat: The sea
Lore: The Dragon Lord, Lạc Long Quân, was the grandson of the Dragon Lord of the Sea, and mythologically one of the creators of the Vietnamese people. While he normally takes the shape of one of the dragons from Asian cultures, he's also able to shapeshift into a handsome young man.

Prior to Vietnam's creation, he was beloved by the people for a series of monster exterminations—a nine-tailed fox, enormous fish, and a monstrous bird, to name a few. Any time the locals beseeched Lạc Long Quân's assistance, he'd do so, gallantly, for no other reason than to keep Vietnam

Dragon Fruit

Pitaya, commonly known as dragon fruit, is the edible fruiting part of a cactus. It has a leathery pink skin that almost functions like a shell around the edible part of the fruit. The spiny spikes on the exterior give the appearance of dragon scales, which inspired its name.

safe. He would use his cunning mind, magic, and his dragon-born strength to slay each threat.

He earned the accolade for being the first king of Vietnam by his involvement with Âu Cơ, a fairy princess and healer of the mountains. Despite irreconcilable differences, the fairy (a creature of fire and the mountains) and the Dragon Lord (a creature of water and the ocean) formed a deep connection and bond. Through their union, Âu Cơ laid an egg from which hatched one hundred people, the first people of Vietnam. Though they both had love in their hearts, the two decided to return to their home regions with half of their children each, who had all rapidly aged to adult men.

Their eldest son, Kinh Dương Vương, is the first ruler of Vietnam. To this day, there are still temples that venerate the legacy of the ancient Hung kings (who are descendants of Kinh Dương Vương).

FAFNIR

Culture of Origin: Nordic
Type: Dragon
Habitat: In a cave with his hoard of gold
Lore: Unlike Nidhogg and Jormungandr, Fafnir did not begin his life as a dragon. Rather, he was a miserly dwarf that killed his father for a gold ring. He coveted and lusted after gold with such wanton greed that he transformed into a dragon to protect his treasure hoard.

Fafnir appears in two Norse epics, *The Song of the Nibelungs* and the *Volsunga Saga*, as a vile beast to be slain by the hero, Sigurd. The Nordic holiday Sigurd's Day celebrates the hero slaying the dragon Fafnir with the aid of a Valkyrie, Brynhildr. It has also been suggested that Fafnir is the dragon mentioned in *Beowulf* (see page 144), the Norse epic poem about the folk hero by the same name, but that is difficult to substantiate.

Fafnir's role in mythology is one of a cautionary tale. His greed gained him much power but ultimately resulted in his downfall and status as the villain. A recurring theme in much of Norse mythology is that when power and resources are concentrated in one area due to the greed of an individual, the many will rise up to depose them. Fafnir may also be the inspiration for one of fiction's most infamous dragons, Smaug from *The Hobbit* (see page 146).

❖ ❖ ❖

THE GREAT FIRE DRAGON / HORNED SERPENT

Culture of Origin: Iroquois Five Nations (Mohawk, Oneida, Onondaga, Cayuga, and Seneca) and other Native American cultures
Type: Serpent / Drake
Habitat: The World Below
Lore: The Great Fire Dragon is a primal spirit in Iroquois mythology. He goes by many names and can shapeshift into many forms. He lives as a malevolent protector of his dominion in the World Below, which is a mythical realm below the one where humans live. He protects the sacred Great White Pine, and in his serpent and dragon form, will sometimes sneak glimpses into the human world through the mirror of a lake. As the Horned Serpent or Great Fire Dragon, he cannot enter this world, lest it immolate in his presence.

He is trickster god, known for getting into trouble, offering bad deals, and generally having nefarious intentions, and can be particularly dangerous to Native American women. While the Horned Serpent (and trickster gods in general) has a bad reputation for causing mischief, it is important to view him in the ecosystem of his mythology. Yes, he caused problems, but the solution at the end usually led to a better outcome for all parties.

There are several different Horned Serpents across different Native American cultures: Uktena (Cherokee); Djodi'kwado (Iroquois); Avanyu (Pueblo); and Gitche-Kenebig (Algonquians). Each iteration has their own local

❖ ❖ ❖

strengths, abilities, weaknesses, and myths unique to each Horned Serpent.

THE GREAT RED DRAGON

Culture of Origin: Unknown
Type: Dragon
Habitat: Apocalypse
Lore: The Great Red Dragon appears in the New Testament's Book of Revelation as the harbinger for the end of the world. The dragon is wreathed in fire, and the line between it being an actual dragon or an interpretation of a demon is vague at best. In some interpretations, this dragon is Satan, the fallen angel Lucifer, himself. If all three of these characters align, it might also be the serpent in the Garden of Eden that tempts young Eve to eat the fruit of the knowledge of good and evil.

The Great Red Dragon resembles the Hydra (see page 98), having seven heads with a crown or diadem perched atop each. Its tail is so long that it can sweep stars from the sky and fling them to Earth. It also has nine horns and can breathe both water and fire. The Great Red Dragon knows that it won't have much time, so it will act quickly and with furious focus. At the end of the world, it will try to devour a sacred child and their mother whole but will ultimately fail. At the end of its rampage, it will be thrown into the abyss.

❖ ❖ ❖

HYDRA

Culture of Origin: Ancient Greek
Type: Dragon
Habitat: The Lernean swamp, commonly known as a portal between the world of the living and the underworld.
Lore: The existence of the Learnean Hydra was popularized in the Greek myth of the Twelve Labors of Hercules. The Learnean Hydra is a beast that starts out with nine heads, one of which is the key to the beast's immortality. The Hydra cannot be slain while this head still lives, and the other eight will regrow if beheaded. Its purpose is to guard the entrance to the underworld, much like Cerberus, the three-headed dog, also featured in Hercules's Labors.

Hercules and his nephew, Iolaus, defeated the Hydra by burning the stumps of the Hydra's necks before they could grow back. This allowed Hercules to whittle down each of the Hydra heads until only its immortal one was left. Once the final head was removed, Hercules and Iolaus buried the immortal head under a boulder so that the beast couldn't resurrect itself.

JORMUNGANDR, THE MIDGARD SERPENT

Culture of Origin: Nordic
Type: Serpent
Habitat: Midgard in Norse mythology is the human realm at the center of the world tree. Midgard is surrounded by seas that wash into other realms, but Jormungandr circles the human realm with his monstrously large body, often depicted from muzzle to tail.

Lore: While Nidhogg's appearance happens first in the Norse mythology canon, the next great dragon to appear is Jormungandr, the Midgard Serpent.

This titanic monster is venomous and often depicted with four legs along its lengthy body. Jormungandr is the son of Loki, and his siblings are the goddess Hel and the wolf Fenrir. Odin, the All-Father god in Norse mythology, fears the beast's size and power and sends the Midgard Serpent to the depths of the ocean. When Jormungandr leaves the oceans to fight Thor during Ragnarök, it will flood Midgard and wipe out many of the people there. Thor and the Midgard Serpent fight to their mutual demise.

KUR

Culture of Origin: Sumerian (modern-day Iraq)
Type: Serpent
Habitat: The bottom of the ocean, "the great below"
Lore: Kur is a curious and ambiguous word from ancient Sumerian. It can be a place (namely, the underworld), represent land in general, or it can be the beast that lurks at the bottom of the ocean.

The myth of Tiâmat's fall and Kur were likely crafted less than a hundred years apart with minor changes. One version of the myth has the god of the sea slaying Kur, and in another the goddess of love and sexuality ends the beast. All versions of the myth begin relatively the same, with Kur abducting Ereshkigal, who would later be known as the goddess of the underworld. If this sounds familiar to a Greek myth, it very much resembles Hades taking the goddess of spring, Persephone, down to the underworld.

Daniel (Biblical)

Daniel's dragon was a living god of Babylon. Like many slayers, Daniel bests the beast through its stomach. He baked a flammable mixture of fat, hair, and pitch (a sticky and incendiary substance derived from pine trees). Once consumed, the dragon exploded.

Whichever Sumerian god or goddess sought to rescue Ereshkigal, they followed Kur out into the sea on a boat to do battle with Kur. Kur throws stones at his slayer and belches fire but is overcome.

Kur had been holding the saltwater away from the fresh, and his death floods the land with toxic water that no plant can grow from. A folk hero, Ninurta, closes the tale with the discovery of agricultural practices to help cultivate crops, mitigating the saltwater corruption of the land.

LA GARGOUILLE

Culture of Origin: French
Type: Dragon
Habitat: Rouen, France
Lore: Commonly anglicized to "gargoyle," this creature's mythology has its roots in medieval France, where the legend first appeared between the seventh and fourteenth centuries. Before then, La Gargouille was a river creature that menaced fishermen along the River Seine. It would forcefully spit geysers of water at passing boats and tip passengers into the river so that it could devour them. Legend has it that it would make its way into the town of Rouen and demand fair maidens for which to eat, although it was known to settle for criminals.

When La Gargouille became too much to bear, Saint Romain, the local bishop, with the assistance of a criminal who was promised freedom as payment for acting as bait, laid a trap for the beast. Once lured, Bishop Romain used his holy clothes and symbol to muzzle the beast and lead it, docile as a lamb, back to town. The town tried to burn La Gargouille and while most of its body turned to ash, its head remained whole since it was heat resistant. The villagers placed the head on the roof of the church as a reminder to all demons that they were unwelcome. It still spits water to this day, except now it keeps rainwater off the masonry of the church's walls.

While this story offers a compelling origin to gargoyles as we know them today, stone architecture on churches and other castle parapets are likely remnants from pagan beliefs rather than this river dragon. La Gargouille is also the name of a cocktail composed of muddled cardamom pods, lime juice, green chartreuse, rum, absinthe, bitters, and simple syrup.

LEVIATHAN

Culture of Origin: Semitic
Type: Serpent
Habitat: Deepest and darkest waters of the ocean; the Mediterranean Sea
Lore: A fearsome creature from the Old Testament that slinks through the depths of the ocean, Leviathan is a sea monster that frightens all other sea monsters. There are many ancient myths of fearsome serpents in the depths of the ocean that surround the world, see Jormungandr (page 98), Apep (page 92), and Kur (page 100). These cosmic serpents will often feast on the souls of the dead, especially on those who were cruel in life.

Legend has it that the creature is nine hundred miles (1,448 km) long with seven heads and hundreds of eyes. Although largely represented as a sea serpent, Leviathan burns hot. He has eyes like bright coals, the ability to breathe

❖ ❖ ❖

fire, has smoke constantly rising from his nostrils, and can boil oceans from his place in their depths. Iron and brass are easily torn apart by his claws, making him fearless in the face of all weaponry. He has durable and tough scales with nary a weak link between them. He possessed an aura so vile that no one can stand its presence for long.

This nasty beast is a feral and ferocious representation of chaos that seeks to destroy all that its maker created. In the end, it is said that either the angels or God himself will kill the beast and that his meat will feed many a hungry belly and his skin will be used to house the destitute.

LOCH NESS MONSTER

Culture of Origin: Scottish
Type: Serpent / Drake
Habitat: Deep rivers and lakes of Scotland
Lore: The Loch Ness Monster (or Nessie as it's been dubbed by modern monster hunters) is a formidable serpentlike creature that lives exclusively in the depths of the fresh water of the lake (*loch* in Scottish) and River Ness.

The first recorded sighting of the Loch Ness Monster was of its banishment at the sign of the cross by Saint Columba in the sixth century CE. The story goes that while journeying into the Scottish Highlands, Saint Columba witnessed a man being menaced by a monstrous beast in the water, the beast having already devoured the man's companion. Saint Columba ran to the victim's aid, rescuing him by making the sign of the cross to cast the monster out. This method of expulsion proved highly effective as the creature was pulled up the River Ness and into the loch, not to be seen again until centuries later.

In truth, the Loch Ness Monster is more likely something like a kelpie or a "water horse." These water spirits were believed to inhabit all bodies of water in Scotland at the time of Saint Columba's banishment of Nessie. This transformation of a neutral water spirit into a monstrous creature trying to devour a man alive was likely an attempt to sway the pagans of the area away from the spirits of the land.

MELUSINE

Culture of Origin: British, French, German, and Luxembourgian
Type: Drake / Dragon
Habitat: Luxurious Castles and Avalon
Lore: Melusine appears in folklore across several countries in Europe, and her legend shifts slightly depending on where the myth takes place—she even has ties to Arthurian legends, supposedly living for a time in Avalon and bearing a

similarity to the Lady of the Lake, the water spirit who gifts Arthur his sacred sword, Excalibur.

The following myth comes from France. Either a water spirit, dragon, or other mythical creature, Melusine was a beautiful and charming woman. A wealthy Count falls in love with her and asks her to marry him. She acquiesces, and the two of them have anywhere from two to ten children together. The Count's domain prospers during his marriage to Melusine, and he builds his love extravagant castles to honor her. As time passes, his family grows suspicious of Melusine's peculiar requests (that she can't be seen on a certain day—usually the holy day of rest—or doing a certain thing—such as bathing herself or the children). Once confronted, Melusine tries to demur, but when pushed, transforms into a dragon and leaves the Count with their children, never to be seen again.

❖ ❖ ❖

Other stories portray her as more of a good-natured, if not mischievous and vengeful, water spirit. A few legends from France depict her as having leathery dragon wings and a tail that she hides from her husband. Some of these myths lean into the medieval European view that dragons were unholy creatures and could not attend church or partake in holy rituals. Melusine is generally seen as a cautionary tale, and the lesson varies depending on who is doing the cautioning.

NIDHOGG

Culture of Origin: Nordic
Type: Dragon
Habitat: Hel, the underworld of the nine realms of the Norse cosmos
Lore: Described as a typical dragon, Nidhogg has black scales and an appetite for chaos. He consumes corpses and any life the roots of the world tree in Norse mythology give him. The dead that wash upon the shores of his domain are the vilest of humanity and deserving of his cruel punishment. His name in Old Norse loosely translates to "evil blow," and he is also called "the great corpse eater." He is tormented by a squirrel that shares the salacious (and likely untrue) gossip it has with the eagle that perches atop the world tree.

Ragnarök, the Norse prophecy for the fall of the gods and end of the world, begins when Nidhogg flies from his mountain home and takes to the land of the living. Modern interpretations have painted Nidhogg as a fearsome creature filled with bloodlust. But some scholars interpret Nidhogg starting Ragnarök as a redemption of his character rather than the beginnings of bloodshed.

Although Nidhogg is an inherently chaotic creature that brings about the end of the Norse gods, he likely wasn't branded as an evil creature. At its core, Norse mythology views chaos a bit differently than other religions, as evident by beloved trickster god, Loki, who is also an agent of chaos. Chaos in Norse mythology is often the crux of change—the causing of havoc shows where systems can be shored up, and a bit of unrest ensures the people are never sitting on their laurels or only doing what is easy.

NÜWA

Culture of Origin: Chinese
Type: Serpent
Habitat: Ancient Earth
Lore: Nüwa is the creator of all humanity in Ancient Chinese mythology. She is usually depicted with a serpent's body and the head of a beautiful woman, but she is also sometimes shown to be more like the nagas from India, where her lower half is a snake's tail and her upper body is humanoid. Strictly speaking, Chinese mythology does not consider Nüwa as a dragon, but her serpentine appearance and powers are similar to other dragon gods profiled in this book.

Nüwa was an immensely powerful goddess that molded the first humans from clay and mud. She also restabilized the pillars of the earth when a battle between the gods threatened to collapse the heavens. She and her brother, Fu Xi, represent the yin and yang of the universe.

QUETZALCOATL / KUKULKAN

Culture of Origin: Aztecan and Mayan
Type: Serpent
Habitat: The heavens
Lore: Like many serpent gods, the plumed serpent Quetzalcoatl was a creator god for the Aztecs in Central America. An earlier version of the plumed serpent in Mayan culture was called Kukulkan, and while a proto version of both these deities likely exists in earlier Olmec culture, Quetzalcoatl and Kukulkan are the most well-known iterations of this plumed serpent.

Along with being the creator of humanity, Quetzalcoatl was a benevolent god of the wind and rain, and a patron of farming, art, and higher learning. He's a pivotal character

to the Aztec canon and embarks on many adventures, which earns him many accolades. He's kind, clever, and curious, despite sometimes getting into particularly violent scuffles with his brother, Tezcatlipoca, god of the night, storms, and conflict.

One story has the brothers doing battle with Tlaltcuhtli, a fearsome earth monster who they ripped in two. From the remains, edible plants sprung from half of them, while the other half, its great spiny back (sometimes likened to that of a crocodile), decomposed into the earth, sky, and mountains.

RYŪJIN

Culture of Origin: Japanese
Type: Dragon
Habitat: Coral castle in the ocean
Lore: Depicted with horns, whiskers like that of a catfish, and a beard, Ryūjin is a Japanese god of the sea and thunder. He has a powerful dragon pearl and uses gems to control the tides from his coral castle beneath the waves. The creatures of the sea all bow to him and fisherman would give him offerings in hopes of calm seas. He's the patron god of an imperial line, with several Japanese emperors supposedly being descended from him.

Ryūjin is often portrayed as a kind and benevolent dragon god, but like many dragon lords and kings, he is not immune to sour moods. One of the most famous myths featuring Ryūjin involves the jellyfish. According to the myth, Ryūjin's daughter became ill and the only cure was a monkey's liver. He sent his servant, the jellyfish, to fetch it. This version of the jellyfish could walk on land and possessed bones and a shell. When the jellyfish found the monkey, it was tricked out of its mission and had to return to the sea empty-handed. Ryūjin was so furious that he beat the bones and shell out of the jellyfish, which is why the invertebrate looks the way it does now.

SATAN

Culture of Origin: Byzantium (Modern-day Istanbul, Turkey)
Type: Drake / Dragon
Habitat: Hell
Lore: Literature in the Middle Ages commonly associated dragons with demons and Satan, although it was usually a metaphor, rather than explicitly stated. One specific story features a dragon named Satan. In the city of Byzantium in 304 CE, Saint Marina (sometimes Saint Margaret) was imprisoned for warding off the advances of the Roman Imperial Governor of the area, Olymbrios. Once in jail,

she suffered torture that tested her faith, but which never once waivered.

After many days, a fissure ruptured in the ground of her cell during an earthquake, and a serpentine dragon, the spirit of Satan himself, slithered out. It had charred skin and was terrible to behold—both in sight and smell. Although serpentine, his features shifted, and he could appear as a man with a flaxen head of hair and golden beard. Gleaming eyes and teeth came through the haze of smoke leaking from his nostrils and sparks lighting his mouth. Satan was as swayed by Saint Marina's beauty as Olymbrios was and offered her whatever she wanted in return for her love and devotion. When her faith held true, even in the presence of this awful creature, she was swallowed whole. Down his gullet, Saint Marina made the sign of the cross, and she exploded the dragon from within. Saint Marina is the saint of childbirth, pregnant women, and the innocents that find themselves unjustly accused.

This tale and the story from the New Testament about the Great Red Dragon (see page 97) have led many people to believe that the devil has a draconic form. Biblical scholars have also assumed that the snake in the Garden of Eden in the creation myth of the Old Testament is also Satan in the form of a lesser dragon.

THE SHAGGY BEAST OF LA FERTÉ-BERNARD

Culture of Origin: British, French, and Spanish
Type: Dragon / Drake
Habitat: The River Huisne

Lore: The French call it La Velue, or the Hairy One; the Spanish, Peluda; and it is commonly known as the Shaggy Beast in English. A monster to its core, this willful creature can be traced to the Bible's Old Testament, in which it was said to have forgone a place on Noah's Ark but still survived the flood. With a host of defensive and offensive animal traits, it is no wonder. The creature is covered by shaggy green fur on its back, quills, and, possibly, the shell of a turtle. It was also described as having four stubby legs topped with claws and a scaled tail. The fact that it could breathe fire is what tips this creature from being a river monster into a dragon.

According to legend, it was hungry for teenage girls and would flood the River Huisne if it didn't get its way. A wise woman advised a gaggle of young villagers that its tail was its weak spot, and when they smashed it, they were able to put an end to the beast's rampage.

TARASQUE

Culture of Origin: French
Type: Dragon
Habitat: The river Rhône between Arles and Avignon
Lore: A popular myth in France from the Middle Ages, most of what we know about Tarasque comes from *The Golden Legend* (ca. 1260) by Jacobus de Voragine. Described as being a beast that was half-fish and half-monster with a spiked turtle shell and descended from Leviathan (see page 102), Tarasque was a sight to behold given how large and long it was. His girth and length were likened to those of an ox and horse, respectively. His hide was thick and nearly

impenetrable, a stalwart defense against onslaught from the local people. With horns and sharpened teeth, he was just as aggressive and fearsome on the attack as he was on the defense. He lived in the river Rhône and would create whirlpools large enough to sink boats.

Saint Martha is often credited with taming the beast. With a holy symbol and holy water, she neutralized Tarasque and then wrapped her girdle around his snout to lead it to the town center, where the locals of Tarascon threw stones at it until it perished.

TIÂMAT

Culture of Origin: Babylonian and Assyrian (modern-day Iraq)
Type: Dragon (although sometimes a serpent)
Habitat: The sea
Lore: Tiâmat is intrinsic to the creation myths of Mesopotamia, commonly recognized as humanity's first established civilization. Babylonia and Assyria were two of the cultures that developed during this time, likely making

Tiâmat one of the very first dragons in existence. While all accounts describe her as fearsome and terrible to behold, she is depicted as both a scaly dragon—with wings and rending claws—and a primordial serpent very similar to Leviathan (see page 102).

An entity of saltwater, her union with Apsû, whose domain was freshwater and chaos (and was likely the inspiration for Apep, see page 92), created the other gods in the Assyrian and Babylonian pantheons. She is both the briny void of pre-existence and the life-giving mother of all. Although she's the mother of other divinities, she was a true creature of chaos and abhorred the gods that represented order. She preferred the company of the more untamed demonic or fiendish creatures that sought to devour men and raise wild animals.

When Apsû was vanquished by a holy spell from Ea (the god of water, wisdom, and medicine), Tiâmat rallied a brood

Susa-No-Wo (Japan)

According to myth, Susa-no-wo came upon a small family of gods weeping for their daughters who had been devoured by the eight-headed serpent of Koshi. Susa-no-wo defeated the serpent and married the last living daughter.

of monstrous clouds and storms to take down the gods, and gathered fiendish allies such as the Viper, the Ravening Dog, the Horned Beast, and the Scorpion-man. Ea's son, Marduk (a god of the sun) did battle with Tiâmat as a champion of the gods. Astride four horses and armed with a spear, foul wind, and lightning bolts, he battled with Tiâmat, who spewed spells at him, and he was so horrified with her army that he trembled and fell to his knees. After a vicious battle, he threw a storm into her mouth and caught her in a net, which temporarily neutralized her. While she was stunned, he ripped her in two. One half of her corpse created the dome of heaven, and the other filled the deep oceans. Separating the two removed the power of the chaotic dark and built the home of the gods.

TYPHON

Culture of Origin: Ancient Greek
Type: Dragon
Habitat: Underworld or active volcanoes
Lore: Titans in Greek mythology were almost always forces of nature and not to be trifled with. Typhon was the offspring of Earth and the Underworld (titans named Gaia and Tartarus, respectively). Typhon himself is described as having two snakes for legs and the body of a man from the hips to his shoulders, on which writhed a hundred serpent heads. He's brightly colored with vibrant reds and greens on his reptilian features and immensely poisonous. Some descriptions give him wings and up to a hundred arms, depending on when the myth was told. He can spew fire from his lips and lob molten stones.

Zeus, the Greek god of the sky and storms, was Typhon's nemesis. The epic battle between the two is told in several different ways. One version even has Typhon trying to hurl an entire mountain at the young storm deity. Zeus would use it as an opportunity to stun Typhon into dropping the mountain on himself, thereby becoming buried beneath it.

Typhon is also at the heart of many Greek monster myths. His union with the terrifying Echidna—a half-goddess/half-serpent monster mother—produced equally fearsome offspring, several of which took after their many-headed patriarch. Some of their children include the three-headed guard dog of the underworld, Cerberus; the dragons who guarded treasures such as the Golden Apples and Golden Fleece; the Lernaean Hydra (see page 98); and a few other horrible offspring.

VRITRA

Culture of Origin: Vedic mythology of India
Type: Serpent
Habitat: Mountains
Lore: Vritra is the malicious firstborn of the dragons that thirsts for all the water of the earth. Vritra is the personification of drought, as it consumes water and holds it in its body, causing a drought with no end in sight. Described as being "shoulder-less," a massive serpent is a modern best guess as to how the creature was depicted. His name literally translates to some version of "obstacle," which sets him up perfectly to be the villain in the myth he stars in.

As the drought worsens and the humans suffer, the Vedic gods elect Indra, a storm god, to fight the serpent. This

resembles other myths of giant serpents battling storm gods, such as Zeus and Typhon (see page 115), Thor and Jormungandr (see page 98), and Marduk and Tiâmat (see page 113).

When Vritra and Indra do battle, it is long and vicious, with Vritra casting spells and Indra wielding lightning, thunder, and hail. Eventually, Indra crushes the dragon's nose to stun it and pops the serpent, swollen with water, with a thunderbolt. From Vritra's body spring seven streams that rush the water back to the people of Earth.

ZMEY GORYNYCH

Culture of Origin: Slavic / Russian
Type: Dragon
Habitat: Mountains and streams
Lore: Zmey is the term for dragons and snakes in Slavic and Russian folklore. Zmey (also Zmei) are usually distinguished by having many heads and tails, can usually speak, and follow European dragon norms: evil creatures with scaly

hide, leathery wings, serpentine neck, two to four legs, and sharp claws. Zmey Gorynych is a dragon that appears in a lot of Russian and Slavic tales that feature traditional folk heroes, such as Dobrynya Nikitch of Kiev, and has the ability to shapeshift into a beautiful man to woo unsuspecting maidens and princesses.

In this folktale, Dobrynya bests the dragon as it bathes in a river, resulting in the zmey pleading for its life. Dobrynya agrees to spare the dragon if it promises to behave, and the zmey, out of spite, immediately breaks its word and whisks a stolen princess (or tsarina) off to the mountains. Dobrynya Nikitch then rescues the princess and returns her home.

ZENNYO RYŪŌ

Culture of Origin: Japanese
Type: Drake / Dragon
Habitat: Kyoto Imperial Palace
Lore: A rain god or goddess in Japan, the mythology surrounding Zennyo has transformed over time. They have been depicted as both masculine and feminine and are heralded as a Dragon King or Queen. They breathe out clouds and can beckon the rain with the sound of their voice. While many rain deities (especially dragons from China, Korea, and Japan) can be temperamental, causing floods as much as ending droughts, Zennyo typically does not flood the areas they have dominion over.

Originally a simple serpent in Japanese Shintoism, Zennyo was also adopted as a Buddhist Dragon Queen when

Buddhism came to Japan. She is described in the Buddhist *Lotus Sutra* as being a clever, witty, and kind young girl who reached enlightenment faster than the Buddha himself. All those around her balked in disbelief, thinking it impossible for anyone—let along a young girl—to outpace the Buddha. No one believed her until she bent the world to her will and changed herself into a man and a buddha, proving them all wrong. Another myth describes how she answered the prayers of a monk in Kyoto during a rainmaking contest sponsored by the Imperial Emperor in 824 CE.

Dragon Breeds from Different Cultures

This chapter lists the different dragon breeds in different cultures, which menace or bless. This is by no means an exhaustive list of every dragon across every culture, but rather a focus on covering the most famous and widely recorded dragons. This short, alphabetized directory covers several types of dragons in folklore across the globe. Among these entries are land spirits, monsters of nightmares, and actual demons.

AMPHIPTERES

Country of Origin: Britain and other parts of Europe
Type: Wyvern
Temperament: Vicious and bloodthirsty
Habitat: Untamed wilderness
Abilities:

* Toxic breath
* Their touch brings disease and plague in humans and livestock
* Flight

Description: An amphiptere is the most literal interpretation of a winged serpent. A winged snake with no legs, its wings can either be feathered or bat wings. It's not described as being particularly large.

Lore: This creature was quite similar to guivres (see page 128) and sometimes considered to be the same creature. They were common in European heraldry, specifically as a banner on particularly vicious armies. It is unclear if they have the same fear of nudity as their French counterparts.

BASILISK / COCKATRICE

Country of Origin: France and Greece
Type: Serpent / Dragon
Temperament: Hostile and vicious
Habitat: Cyrene, Greece; Libya, Africa; and the Middle East
Abilities:

* Can kill creatures through eye contact

- The French version, the basilic, petrifies its victims
- Breathes fire and spits venom, which it uses to knock birds from the sky
- Produces noxious fumes
- Produces hydrophobia (or fear of water) in humans that can drive them insane
- Withers plants and infects the soil
- Has a presence so withering that it can break boulders
- Makes a hissing sound so awful, that other creatures flee from it
- Basilisk blood is a key component in the alchemy recipe for Spanish Gold

Description: Original accounts of this beast make note that while it may boast a host of deadly abilities, it is not very large, only nine to twelve inches (23 to 30 cm) long. It is a small, scaly snake, not dissimilar in size and coloring to a garden snake. Later accounts describe a basilisk as being quite a bit larger. Due to the way they're created, basilisks are sometimes given bird or chicken-like qualities (feathers and up to eight chicken legs).

Lore: There are many fictional representations of this creature—it even showed up in William Shakespeare's works—but its original description came from Pliny the Elder, who reported the creature as being real and fearsome in his most famous work, *Natural Histories*.

To create a basilisk, you need a seven-year-old chicken egg warmed by a toad for ten years. To avoid the salted earth and certain doom the basilisk promises, keep a proud and crowing rooster close, as the beast cannot stand the sound. If an encounter is inevitable, you may be able to use its deathly stare by holding out a crystal and showing it its reflection. A weasel's musk and bite are also things this small but fierce creature tries to avoid.

BOLLA AND KULSHEDRA

Country of Origin: Albania
Type: Wyvern / Drake
Temperament: Wicked and hungry
Habitat: Lives in or near water, depending on the type of Kulshedra
Abilities:

* Flight
* Shapeshifting
* Spark spitter

Description: Kulshedra is usually portrayed as a feminine creature. Depending on the region, kulshedra can either be a wyvern-like creature that streaks through the sky with sparks in her teeth or a withering and unsightly hag with a bent spine. In her wyvern form, she can have many heads.

Lore: Like a demonic butterfly, a kulshedra starts as a bolla and evolves with the proper diet and conditions. Bollas are predatory serpents that slither with their eyes closed for most of the year and hibernate for the winter months. The one exception is on Saint George's Day (April 23), when she opens her eyes and seeks out a human. The first person she sees will be killed and devoured. After twelve years—and twelve human souls consumed—a bolla evolves into a kulshedra.

Kulshedras are Baba Yaga–like demonic villains in many Albanian folktales. They make their home near clean water sources then, over time, putrefies them with their presence. When displeased, or if the fancy strikes, they'll incite weather-related catastrophes like drought, floods, and earthquakes. A true being of chaos, they thrive in human anguish but find that suffering can be so much sweeter when their victims bring it on themselves. Kulshedras love tormenting humans, although their hunger to cause suffering can be abated for a time with a willing human sacrifice.

DRAGON KINGS

Country of Origin: China, Vietnam, and Japan
Type: Dragon / Drake
Temperament: Benevolent benefactor
Habitat: Enormous underwater castles constructed from crystals or pearls
Abilities:

* Shapeshifting
* Controlling thunder and rainfall
* Riding waves at top speed
* Flight

Description: Accounts describe them as being immensely handsome or beautiful in their human form, with a durable scale hide in their dragon form.

Lore: Dragon Kings are gods among dragons and key characters in Asian folklore. They live in castles made of crystals or pearls at the bottom of the ocean or the deepest lakes, and they preside over courts of sea creatures, shapeshifters, and other lesser dragons. They were revered and held great responsibility to their regions, where they would care for bodies of water and bestow rainfall. They're extremely powerful, but frequently require help and rely upon human kindness to solve some of their problems. They pay for these favors with lavish gifts, and there are a few stories where dragon princesses fall in love with their human rescuers. One such Japanese folktale involves a fisherman rescuing a turtle from the torment of mischievous children. The turtle thanks him for his kindness and brings him to the

Dragon King's palace. Later, she transforms, and it's revealed that she's a Dragon Princess.

Another Chinese folktale describes a young traveling merchant that stumbles across a weeping shepherdess. She tells him that she's actually a dragon princess and laments that her husband (a lesser Dragon King) and his family treat her poorly. She would leave, but they will not allow her to return to her father (a greater Dragon King along the coast). The merchant tells the princess's father and her uncle lays ruin to her husband's kingdom to rescue his niece. The merchant and the princess eventually wed, and in time, he ascends to become a Dragon King by her side.

Both folktales demonstrate how doing favors for benevolent Dragon Kings can bring virtuous mortals untold good fortune and happiness.

DRAKON

Country of Origin: Ancient Greece
Type: Usually serpentine, but not always
Temperament: Ferocious
Habitat: Caves
Abilities:

* Poisonous, or having poison spit
* Immunity to poison and venom

Description: A monstrous plumed serpent with a small mouth and small fangs, the strength of this dragon comes from its lashing tail rather than its bite with needle-like teeth. A narrow windpipe makes it one of the few dragons who don't try to swallow their prey whole.

❖ ❖ ❖

Lore: Ancient Greek myths are rife with dragons and dragon-like creatures causing mayhem and destruction. This is partially due to the expansiveness of the definition, by Ancient Greek standards. The Greek word for dragon is drakon, which is how we know to categorize the winged and flying saurian alongside the world-sized serpents. Greeks also used the words draconata or draco as well (according to *Etymologies* by Isidore of Seville).

Drakons as a breed of dragon are precocious hunters that would use their length to their advantage. They would hide in the brush along well-worn paths, and once their prey was close, a drakon would dart out and tangle their prey's legs to trip the animal then wrap their serpentine bodies around its throat.

A drakon's brain was the only known location for draconite, a glimmering and precious stone that was a valuable ingredient for magicians and alchemists. This stone could only be retrieved from a living drakon (most likely one that had been tricked into slumber). If removed from a dead drakon, it would no longer have the quality of a gem and be rendered useless for the magician's purposes.

GUIVRE

Country of Origin: France
Type: Wyvern
Temperament: Aggressive, skunk-like, and bashful
Habitat: Damp and wet wilderness
Abilities:

* Toxic breath

* Their touch causes disease and plague in humans and livestock
* Flight

Description: A serpentine reptilian beast that sometimes has leathery, bat-like wings.

Lore: Sometimes also named a "wivre," these French dragons are harbingers of disease, plague, and pestilence. They are territorial by default and attack humans on sight. Deadly to the touch and with a noxious breath, these skunk-like creatures demanded a wide berth if the traveler who saw them wanted to survive. On the off chance a person encountered a guivre, the best practice would be to strip naked. The lonely and isolated creature was said to be extremely bashful and would avert its eyes at the sight of human nudity, at which point a wise would-be victim would run away to safety.

IMUGIS

Country of Origin: Korea
Type: Serpent
Temperament: Kind and benevolent or beastly
Habitat: Bodies of water
Abilities: Long life span
Description: They have serpentine bodies that resemble the Korean celestial dragons, yeong (see page 140), but are much smaller with stunted arms and the beginning nubs of horns.

Lore: Imugi, which literally translates to "great lizard" in Korean, are juvenile yeong. They can be quite animalistic and beastly before they ascend to their final form. This is likely due to the belief that some imugis can be cursed yeong rather than juvenile yeong. To live out their potential, they must live for at least a thousand years and accomplish various tasks to acquire their legs, the ability to fly, and the ability to hold a dragon pearl. These tasks are meant to show their courage and compassion and will sometimes involve living a millennium each in the skies, seas, or among the people. Like yeongs, seeing an imugi is considered a lucky boon.

LÓNG

Country of Origin: China
Type: Dragon
Temperament: Generous yet temperamental
Habitat: Large bodies of water (oceans, rivers, lakes, etc.), with the most illustrious lóngs living in crystal castles at the bottom of the ocean or as Dragon Kings (see page 126)
Abilities:

* Control of the weather, power of thunder and lightning, and holding dominion over water
* Can breathe clouds and exhale water with Qi, or the energy of the universe
* Flight
* Speech
* Can create dragon fire

Description: Lóngs have a long, thick serpentine body with four legs. They are also described with the specific physical features of nine animals, such as the ears of an ox and the paws of a tiger, because nine is a sacred number. Sometimes,

Year of The Dragon

The Chinese zodiac attributes an animal to each year
of its twelve-year cycle before starting it anew. While
all the animals have their strengths, and while there is
much more to the Chinese zodiac than the year you are
born, the years of the dragon are coveted. Hospitals see
increased births in those years, and babies born under
this Chinese zodiac sign are said to be destined for
greatness and blessed with charm.

they are described as having a magical orb tucked under
their chin. The different colors of lóngs are also symbolic of
other things when rendered artistically or featured in myths.
For example, the red dragon is associated with good fortune
and happiness, the white dragon with virtue and death, and
the yellow dragon with power and wealth.

Lore: There is no single origin to lóngs in China, and their
lore has evolved over the centuries. Lóngs are some of the
first primordial beings to inhabit the world in many different
iterations of Chinese creation myths. Lóngs are usually good-
natured and symbols of good luck and prosperity. However,
just like a summer storm, they can be temperamental and lash
out when disrespected. Respect can be shown by uncommon
kindness toward animals or the lóng in question, or by gifts of
jade, pearls, or tasty swallows. To ward off an irritable lóng, it
was suggested to keep iron at hand or a branch from a grafted

tree of which they hate the smell and sap. Lóngs are strongly associated with bodies of water and rain. The qi of a lóng is associated with masculine energy (yang) and is balanced by the feminine energy (yin) of the phoenix.

MO'O

Country of Origin: United States
Type: Drake
Temperament: Gentle giant
Habitat: Coral reefs, caves, and shallow pools of freshwater
Abilities:

* Control and manipulate the weather
* Shapeshifting into humans or geckos

Description: A 30-foot-long (9 m) scaled creature with fangs and four feet or flippered legs. Other accounts have them being mountainous in size or as small as a gecko. Interestingly, there are no reptiles or amphibians native to Hawaii, so the origin of the mo'o's appearance is a mystery.

Lore: Sometimes little more than a beast, other times they're intelligent, named, and participate in human culture. Whether water spirits or water gods, mo'o are pivotal characters in Hawaiian mythology. In their human forms, mo'o are usually described as breathtakingly beautiful women. Mo'o have been known to take care of fish and other water creatures and will love people who care for aquatic life and those who don't put them or their habitats in jeopardy. They protect the land fiercely and punish humans who disrespect it. When a mo'o dies, its body petrifies at its final resting point and becomes part of the land.

They're territorial creatures, so if you stumble upon their lair, which is described as a fresh watering hole with an unsettling yellow tinge to the plants and water, it's best to leave the creature unprovoked.

NAGA

Country of Origin: India, Indonesia, Malaysia, and Thailand
Type: Wyvern / Drake
Temperament: Difficult to describe
Habitat: Underwater or subterranean palaces
Abilities:

* Control over the weather
* Ethereal beauty
* Shapeshifting

Description: Nagas come in several different forms and have evolved over time and cultural exchanges. According to some, they have the lower half of a snake and the upper body of a human. Other myths describe them as a normal snake that guards jewels. There are myths that portray them as winged sea-dragons with the lower half of a snake, the upper body of a human, and potentially the head of an ox. And other sources claim they are multi-headed land and sea dragons that guard temples in Indonesia and Thailand or terrorize fisherman in Malaysia.

Lore: The name naga can apply to several different types of creatures in India, Malaysia, Indonesia, and Thailand. Naga refers to the male version of these creatures, whereas the females are called naginis.

Some nagas are human-like, neither fully malicious nor fully benevolent toward their fellow living creatures, while others, like those of Indonesia, Thailand, and West Malaysia, are terrifying monsters.

Indian nagas, which are the most common representation, are like people in the sense that they are multidimensional. Their one true enemy is the garuda in India, a mythical bird that seeks to release the water they hold from their bodies. The mythical bird's relentless quest for the naga's destruction marks the two species as mortal enemies. Protection from the garuda is also one of the reasons they elect their king: Anata-Shsha in Vedic mythology, Karkotaka in Hindu mythology, and Muchalinda in Buddhist mythology. Muchalinda has strong ties to the Buddha and can transform into an enormous king cobra serpent.

❖ ❖ ❖

SNALLYGASTER

Country of Origin: United States
Type: Wyvern
Temperament: Ferocious
Habitat: Frederick County, Maryland (and the wild woods and mountains of the rest of Appalachia)
Abilities:

* Flight
* Goring beak

Description: A reptilian bird with a massive wingspan, sharp beak or snout, hooked talons, a single massive eye in the center of their forehead, a tentacle-like tongue, and teeth like knives.

Lore: Derived from the German *schnell geist* which translates to "quick ghost," the snallygaster is an Appalachian cryptid. Their form is reminiscent of the Chinese lóng, where they borrow many different elements from other creatures. Snallygasters as we know them now originated

in the early 1900s as a local superstition, although earlier accounts of the area described an abundance of dragon-like creatures. Their conception, and those of other early American cryptids, came from German immigrants (who would have known of other European dragon lore) who likely meshed their understanding of dragons to local Native American folklore.

TANIWHA

Country of Origin: New Zealand
Type: Drake / Dragon
Temperament: Ranges from bloodthirsty to affectionate and protective
Habitat: Large bodies of water (fresh or salt) and caves
Abilities:

* Shapeshifter

* Flight

Rushing Raging Man (Japanese)

A folk hero comes across a grieving family and promises vengeance on the eight-headed Serpent of Koshi that has devoured their daughters. They distill a potent liquor and leave enough barrels for each head to consume, and once the dragon passes out drunk, Rushing Raging Man stabs it with such force that his sword breaks.

Description: They have bright blazing eyes, razor-sharp fangs, and a whip-like tail. They may have been based on the longfin eel, which is a fierce predator with a slightly gruesome appearance. Although they are shapeshifters, they prefer the forms of sea creatures. Some taniwhas begin their lives as other sea creatures, grow to enormous sizes, and adopt dragon-like features. For example, one started out as a shark that grew to the size of a whale, and then later, as it aged, adopted a scaled hide, wings, and a birdlike snout.

Lore: The taniwha are multifaceted and powerful water spirits in Māori folklore. They could either be strongly bonded to humans or inclined to devour them whole. There are a few stories of taniwha eating people only to get their stomachs sliced open and the live bodies of their victims tumble out. Other stories link them as guides and beloved companions to Māori chiefs. There are also tales of a taniwha as a dolphin that would guide boats into the harbor.

TATSU/RYU

Country of Origin: Japan
Type: Dragon
Temperament: Willful, stubborn, empathetic, and full of energy
Habitat: Mountains, wilderness, the sea, lakes, rivers, or other bodies of water
Abilities:

* Controls water
* Strong ryu can control the tides

Description: Traditional tatsu look like other Eastern dragons, with long, serpentine bodies. You can distinguish Japanese tatsus from other dragons in Asian cultures by their number of toes (Japanese tatsu/ryu have three, Korean yeongs have four, and lóngs have four to five).

Lore: Tatsu and ryu generally refer to the same type of creature, with tatsu being the earlier and more traditional form of the word, and ryu being a more modern version. Another interpretation is that tatsu refer strictly to Japanese dragons and folklore, and ryu can more commonly refer to something akin to a European dragon. Tatsu is also part of an older dialect of Japanese and tied to the Japanese astrology sign of the "dragon." The Japanese zodiac replicates the same twelve-year cycle of the Chinese zodiac.

Tatsu are neither good nor bad, but rather extremely powerful creatures that enjoy treasures and usually don't bother too much with human dalliances. Like lóng (see page 130), they'll gift travelers with treasure. They do also appreciate worship and have been known to grant rain during droughts.

Ryu and tatsu are common staples at Buddhist temples and Shinto shrines in Japan. One popular Buddhist Sutra (or religious text) called the *Lotus Sutra* heavily involves dragons, which in part likely contributed to Buddhist dragon shrines across Japan.

❖ ❖ ❖

TATZELWURM / STOLLENWURM

Country of Origin: Switzerland or Albania
Type: Wyrm
Temperament: Skittish and will only attack in defense
Habitat: Mountainous regions, specifically the Swiss Alps
Abilities:

* Noxious breath
* Rarely, the ability to spit fire
* So hot that it can melt sand into glass

Description: A long, reptilian body—sometimes with two to four short legs depending on the account—with a serpentine tail and a long neck with the face of a cat. Accounts of their size vary from as little as one foot long to as large as a house. It will sometimes rear up on its hind legs or tail to appear taller. They can either be white or black, the black ones being more common, and the white ones having a crest atop their heads that looks a bit like a crown. Stollenwurms are typically described as being larger than tatzelwurms.

Lore: As early as the late 1600s and as late as the 1950s, tatzewurms and stollenwurms have been lurking in the Alps. Occasional interactions with humans depict these creatures as behaving like wild animals. Many hikers and hunters across the centuries have witnessed this frightful creature, but it rarely makes use of its ability to spew fire or poison and will only resort to attacking humans to flee from them. At higher altitudes, they have been known to terrorize dairy farmers by suckling on their cows in the middle of the night. They could, potentially, be related to the basilisk (see page 122).

YEONG

Country of Origin: Korea
Type: Dragon
Temperament: Kind and benevolent
Habitat: Bodies of water
Abilities:

* Long life span
* Flight
* Ability to make rain
* Shapeshifting and manipulating its size
* Invisibility

Description: Very similar to Chinese lóngs (see page 130) and Japanese tatsus (see page 137) with the addition of horns and a feathered tail. They carry a version of the dragon pearl that can manifest the greatest desires of the dragon that holds it. Yeongs usually have four or five claws, although one tale told of a particularly prideful yeong who had, to its detriment, seven claws. On their backs are eighty-one shimmering scales (which is the sacred number nine multiplied by itself). Thirty-six scales are sometimes "evil" scales that go against the grain of the rest of their scales.

Lore: Yeongs are wise elders that protect people against evil spirits. Seeing these creatures will bring luck. One potential way to see a yeong is via a rainbow, which is believed to be the path they take as they ascend to heaven. They're weakened by iron; therefore ambitious individuals seeking to harm yeongs can drive iron spikes into particular points along dragon lines (or lines that carry energy across the earth). Yeongs are deeply spiritual creatures that exist half in the human world and half in other worlds and as such, can rarely be seen in their entirety.

Dragons in Fiction

Modern audiences love the majesty of dragons, and nothing so effectively immerses audiences into fantasy worldbuilding than a robust spin on the medieval bestiary. Many of the dragons represented in this chapter will be of the European archetype—fire breathing dragons or wyverns meant to strike fear and awe into the hearts and minds of readers or watchers. However, just because European dragons are most recognizable and prevalent in modern media, each individual piece of media is presented chronologically as I examine the most famous and iconic dragons in fiction. Because there are a lot of intriguing dragons to cover, some of the less formative works will be represented in groups.

BEOWULF (650–800 CE)

Beowulf is an old Norse epic of a legendary Danish ruler. It is a staple of classical literature. Beloved by his people and a valiant warrior to-boot, Beowulf's epic poem involves many monsters and ends with a battle between Beowulf and a dragon. After slaying the monster Grendel and Grendel's mother, Beowulf ascends the throne. Later, he protects his people from the wrath of a vengeful dragon after a member of Beowulf's community steals a golden cup from the dragon's hoard.

Beowulf leads a troupe of the bravest men to face the nameless dragon, which is described as a sleek, black, tusked, airborne creature of spite that spits fire and poison. The dragon, known as the "destroyer of nations," revels in the fear he causes and wants nothing more than for the humans to descend into anarchy and war. The beast terrifies nearly all of Beowulf's men into leaving and makes short work of the others who remain.

With the help of his sole living companion, Wiglaf, Beowulf lands a killing blow on the monster, but not before the monster does the same. Beowulf dies from the poison, and his people burn him, the dragon, and the dragon's cursed treasure to honor the ruler they adored.

Folklore Sources Referenced

Beowulf occupies a unique space of being both a folklore source *and* referencing the sacred texts of Norse mythology simultaneously. Many of the themes and common traits in the Norse epics like *Beowulf* likely

Ketil Trout (Norse)

In the *Saga of Ketil Trout*, the titular character encounters a flying reptile with a deadly tail and sparks burning in its eyes and mouth. He cleaves the beast in two by striking its coiling body.

influenced representations of dragons in modern European literature. *Beowulf's* popularity certainly assisted in the proliferation of certain stereotypes.

Additionally, the cursed treasure of a dragon's hoard is explained in *Beowulf* in ways that other pieces of folklore don't delve into as thoroughly. The treasure itself is cursed because of the greed required to accumulate it. It symbolizes distrust and a lack of social cohesion. If a dragon has a hoard of treasure—especially in the case of Fafnir, who was transformed into a dragon by his greed—it means that other people have had to do without.

Cultural Context

Beowulf's impact on fantasy and fiction has made it a staple in many literature classes. Ironically, it is commonly believed that the epic saga was not widely read in the Middle Ages despite its modern popularity. Some classical literature specialists assert that the dragon in *Beowulf* is a version of Fafnir (see page 95). For example, Fafnir's lust for treasure and treasure hoarding is replicated in the nameless dragon in *Beowulf*. Both Norse dragons are what inspired the well-known trope of dragons' greed in literature.

THE HOBBIT (1937) AND THE LORD OF THE RINGS (1954)

We may have dragons to thank for arguably one of the most well-known, beloved, and prolific fantasy series of the modern era. *The Hobbit* (1937) and the follow-up trilogy, *The Lord of the Rings* (1954) is a fantasy series set in the mythical land of Middle Earth, which is resplendent with fantastical creatures and humanoids.

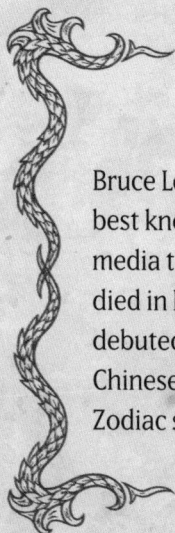

The Dragon, Bruce Lee

Bruce Lee was a Chinese-American action movie star best known for rewriting Asian stereotypes in American media through his prodigious martial arts skills. Lee died in his thirties, and his final film, *Enter the Dragon*, debuted in theaters after he died. His stage name in Chinese translates to "Little Dragon," and his Chinese Zodiac sign was the dragon.

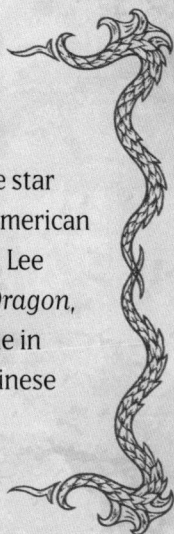

There are both proper dragons and wyverns in author J.R.R. Tolkien's works. The most famous traditional dragon would be Smaug, the infamous dragon sitting on a hoard of treasure in his mountain lair, and one of the main antagonists in *The Hobbit*. Tolkien's illustrations of Smaug depict a red dragon with smoking nostrils, a long serpentlike body and tail, four legs, the ears of a deer, and bat-like wings. Renowned for his brutality and greed, Smaug is a formidable foe who can only be slain by wounding a soft spot on his belly. Smaug is capable of speech, has sharpened senses, and a deep-seated pride that turns out to be his undoing.

The other dragon-like creatures in Middle Earth are the winged mounts of the ring wraiths, sometimes called fell beasts. These beasts are all described as having uniquely terrible features and are usually represented as some sort of flying dinosaur or wyvern-type creature. They do not speak or breathe fire and are not nearly as intelligent as Smaug. They are little more than ancient mounts intended to instill horror.

Folklore Sources Referenced

A young J.R.R. Tolkien had a blossoming interest in dragons, seeded by his love of Norse mythology. Much of the mythology of Middle Earth is based off the beings and ancient poetry of the Norse people. The two dragons that Tolkien cited as being his inspiration for Smaug are Fafnir (see page 95) and the dragon from *Beowulf* (see page 144), who many also believe to be Fafnir.

Tolkien's most famous works function with a very binary view of good and evil. While there are elements that show

❖ ❖ ❖

nuance to the two (particularly the actions of humans throughout his books), the world that Tolkien creates in *The Lord of the Rings* offers a sharp divide between the binary of good and evil. This replicates the medieval view of dragons being creatures akin to demons, beings outside redemption. In this view, all dragons are creatures filled with malice bent on destruction. While Smaug is a selfish agent of chaos, the fell beasts are evil by nature and utterly irredeemable.

Cultural Context

Tolkien's work is a pillar of the fantasy genre. His worldbuilding and characters are so popular that his works have been adapted into several movies, a musical, animation, and a prestige television series. Delighted fans can visit their favorite film locations from Peter Jackson's *The Lord of the Rings* trilogy in New Zealand. The sets are immortalized as a preserved pocket of Middle Earth for tourists.

Aside from Tolkien's extensive adaptations and boon to tourism, Smaug is, for all intents and purposes, the parent of most malevolent modern-day dragons. If a dragon is intelligent enough to talk and unkind by nature, they are likely inspired by the villain that Tolkien created. The portrayal of dragons as being chaotic evil creatures has existed since 400 CE, but Tolkien certainly ensured that it remained a popular interpretation. Much of dragon canon (their hoards, their abilities, their appearance) can be interpreted as based off Tolkien's writing as well.

Tolkien also made dragons—and pardon the lack of eloquence here—extremely cool. Incredibly powerful and

Godzilla and Other Kaiju

Godzilla is a gigantic amphibious monster that slumbered in the Pacific until it was awoken by nuclear testing. Radiation strengthened the creature, and with its new power, it set out to level Japan in a furious rampage. The big guy makes his first appearance in the 1954 film written and directed by Ishiro Honda that is a metaphor for the devastating consequences of nuclear power. The monster movie's practical effects and titular character are famous to this day, and Godzilla has gone on to be the star of nearly forty feature films since its debut in 1954.

Godzilla is also attributed as being the cultural parent of kaiju, or other building-sized monsters that rampage through cities. Kaiju, which literally translates to "strange beast" in Japanese, can be prehistoric monsters, aliens, or have any number of other origins.

Godzilla and many other kaiju are not technically dragons, but some of them do contain dragon traits that have been covered in this book. Additionally, while nuclear radiation and pollution from the industrial revolution aren't quite the same, there is a thematic connection in the alignment of dragons and Godzilla to poisonous substances.

silver-tongued with a mind just as sharp, it is hard not to fall in love with the cartoonishly evil visage of Smaug. Interestingly, this sets dragons up to be the antagonist in subsequent dragon-related media. In later works of fiction, creators attempted to build complex narratives around dragons or characters that are intimately associated with dragons.

DUNGEONS & DRAGONS (D&D)

Dungeons & Dragons (commonly referred to as D&D) is a tabletop roleplaying game first published in 1974 by Gary Gygax's game publisher, Tactical Studies Rules (TSR). The original game was called Castle & Crusade Society since it was connected to larger wargames. When the game was officially published, Gygax ran a few alliterative ideas by his daughter before deciding on Dungeons & Dragons.

For gameplay, players create characters and build a story through interactions with other players. The dungeon

master enforces the rules, nudges players towards solving mysteries, describes the setting, and acts on behalf of all the non-player characters (NPCs) to move the narrative along. As with all their monsters, D&D publishes books that provide players and dungeon masters with abilities, strengths, weaknesses, and behaviors.

D&D has experienced a surge in popularity through representation in popular shows like *Stranger Things* (2016) and *Community* (2009), as well as through live-play podcasts and livestreams such as *The Adventure Zone*, *Critical Role*, and *Dimension 20*. The game has also inspired two films, *Dungeons & Dragons* (2000) and *Dungeons & Dragons: Honor Among Thieves* (2023).

Folklore Sources Referenced

The dragons that appear in D&D are very similar to the dragons from Norse mythology. This is because Tolkien's works inspired the early games that Gygax was developing. Additionally, there are many types of dragons in D&D, and they come in a range of different species which are usually named after a color, gemstone or precious metal, or species hybrids—such as fairy or turtle. The different colors of dragons replicate those in Chinese mythology, although it's not an exact comparison.

Other types of creatures (nagas, wyverns, drakes, basilisks, and other dragon-like monsters mentioned in this book) do appear in D&D bestiaries, demonstrating a commitment to dragons under all their names and appearances.

Cultural Context

As D&D gained wide popularity amongst young players in the 1980s, it got caught up in the "Satanic Panic," a moral panic in which parents thought the tabletop game was a gateway to satanism and could end in something as dire as human sacrifice. The basis for D&D being a gateway to ritual sacrifice has long since been debunked, but it is interesting that medieval Europeans and suburban parents, hundreds of years and miles apart, believed the same thing about a mythical creature.

Dungeons & Dragons has, for decades, been a playground for people who enjoy fantasy and dragons. The makers have published numerous books, built out extensive lore, and created a structure of rules for fantastical creatures and magic. The style of play has made it easier for everyone to

Lucky Dragon 5

This Japanese fishing boat counted their Radio Officer as among the first victims of the atomic bomb when nuclear testing exceeded expectations and safety precautions. A cloud of irradiated particles and coral carried on the wind overcame the fishing boat, and it was days before the vessel returned to shore. All the members suffered from radiation sickness, with one member dying. Their heartbreaking story is part of the inspiration for Godzilla (see page 149).

co-create in the same sandbox, and the game's open gaming license allows players to use their own rule set and structure to create their own stories.

GAME OF THRONES (1996)

In 1996, George R.R. Martin released the first book in the A Song of Ice and Fire series, which showrunners David Benioff and D. B. Weiss would later adapt into a prestige television series for HBO titled *Game of Thrones* (2011–2019). Set in the fantasy world of Westeros, dragons and their return to the world is a key plot point for the series and subsequent HBO spinoff series *House of the Dragon* (2022–present). The world of Westeros is rife with mythical creatures, political intrigue, and is inspired by real historical events.

The dragons in Martin's world are tied to one noble house, Targaryen, whose family crest is a three-headed dragon. Dragons are depicted as having a close relationship with the members of the Targaryen family, protecting them, obeying their commands, and flying them into battle. One fan favorite character, Daenerys Targaryen, is referred to as the "Mother of Dragons" throughout the series. In a series that spans centuries, pinning down a single throughline plot for dragons is difficult, but fans of the shows and books continually return for the famed fantasy beasts.

Folklore Sources Referenced

Martin's dragons have a very specific lore attached to them. They are based mostly on European dragons, but their appearance is technically closer to a wyvern. These dragons have an interesting link to stones: their eggs petrify as the magic that animates them dissipates, similar to the myth that dragon stones in the heads of living dragons would transform from gem to common rock if cut from a dead dragon.

There are actual wyverns in Martin's world, and while they function as the basis for Targaryen dragons, they're a bit smaller and don't breathe fire. They're also described as more beast-like and less intelligent or loyal than the creatures they yielded.

Cultural Context

Dragons have been beloved by fantasy enthusiasts for as long as they've been interwoven into the genre, but the Game of Thrones series captured such a wide audience that it launched the genre and dragons into the highest echelons of pop culture and is credited with inspiring people to take an interest in the fantasy genre. While Tolkien may have written the original works of dragons in the periphery, Martin's works used them as central figures.

The final episode of *Game of Thrones* garnered 19.3 million viewers. The success of the original television series and its spinoff has fans eagerly (and somewhat impatiently) awaiting the final books in Martin's series.

DRAGONS IN MODERN MEDIA

Dragons are as prolific in modern media as they are in ancient texts. They are a staple in fantasy genres across age groups and are a general crowd pleaser for audiences in the many books, television shows, and movies they appear in.

Animated children's movies and television series like *Quest for Camelot* (1998), *Dragon Tales* (1999–2005), *The Dragon Prince* (2018–present), *How to Train Your Dragon* (2018–2025), and many more portray dragons as companions to humans. These dragons can be sassy, but in general bond with the human characters and help them grow. They add a layer of whimsy and engage audiences' curiosity for the mystical and unknown, a bit like the bestiaries of the Middle Ages.

Examples of dragons in young adult literature and media include beloved fantasy properties such as Dragonriders of Pern (1968–2024), The Inheritance Cycle (2002–2011) by Christopher Paolini, and Harry Potter series (1997–2007) by J. K. Rowling with their subsequent movie spinoffs. Dragons for this age group are still deadly, and the stakes are a little more intense than in children's media. They can either be pivotal to the plot or fantastical creatures that contribute to world building.

Recently, dragons have become a popular addition to the "romantasy" genre (a hybrid of romance and fantasy). The most popular example is Rebecca Yarros's best-selling The Empyrean series (2023–present) that focuses on a school of dragon-riders and features characters with psychic connections to their dragons. Dragons in this genre are more likely to indulge their desire to devour people whole who irritate them, since it is a genre exclusively for adults.

Folklore Sources Referenced

Harry Potter's dragons draw on the fact that different breeds come from different areas, though they're primarily based in Europe. This reflects a larger trend of European dragon lore influencing contemporary representations of dragons. Modern depictions often physically resemble European dragons with leathery wings, a hardened hide, sharp claws or talons, and fiery breath. These representations even incorporate the attitudes and ideas about dragons prevalent in European folklore. For example, How to Train Your Dragon draws heavily on the animosity between Nordic folk heroes and the dragons of Norse myths, featuring the human characters as Vikings who hunt down dragons.

In some of these representations, dragons are personified and other times they're more akin to vastly intelligent animals. The dragons in Fourth Wing resemble dragon kings from Asian cultures in the sense that they speak, have a hierarchy independent of humans, and can be kind but also grumpy and temperamental. However, their distinct tails replicate some European dragons.

❖ ❖ ❖

Unlike the European dragons of the Middle Ages, most dragons in modern media are not portrayed as inherently evil. Frequently, different pieces of media will pick and choose interesting elements from different folklore to inform the worlds they create.

Cultural Context

Modern representations of dragons are a testament to this mythic creature's lasting popularity. Series based around dragons cultivate large fanbases and tend to carry on for decades. The Dragonlance series, originally published as D&D properties, includes over 190 titles and has been recognized by many bestseller lists. The Inheritance Cycle was originally meant to be a trilogy but grew into four books plus a few spin-offs, with room to grow from there.

While some dragons in modern media are still depicted as evil or immoral creatures, other newer adaptations have cast them in a heroic, or at the very least, less villainous light. In fact, they have become prominent, lovable characters in series such as *How to Train Your Dragon, Shrek,* and The Empyrean Series. This shifting attitude and continued interest in dragons has led to an influx of dragon-centered media and dragon-infused fantasy. Creators become immersed in their worlds and can't resist building out epic tales surrounding this incredible fantasy creature.

Conclusion

There are a smaller amount of unknowns in the modern world, fewer areas unexplored, and far less corners for dragons to hide in. However, if dragons are at the beginning of many human cultures, perhaps we hold dragons within ourselves. A dragon is a monstrous task put before us, something on our to-do list to slay. We could be the dragon that spearheads positive change in our communities or burns down the systems that no longer serve us. Dragons can be something as simple as our belief in the impossible or an answered prayer for rain.

From their beginnings in creation myths to their villainy in medieval literature to their more heroic rebranding in modern media, dragons have continued to awe and fascinate. Although the dragons may be gone from the map's edge, we can still find them if we look hard enough.

Dragon Monuments and Lairs Around the World

③

⑥

①

⑦

Dragon Monuments

Dragon Lairs

Dragons can be found beyond the pages of books, for those daring enough to look. From a temple in Mexico to wetlands in Greece, this appendix shares popular dragon monuments and rumored lairs around the world. Admire the beautiful architecture that celebrates the power of these magnificent creatures or venture into a their lairs for a chance to spot the famous dragons of lore.

DRAGON MONUMENTS

① Temple to Quetzalcoatl

Location: Teotihuacan, Modern Day Mexico

Established around 100–150 BCE and thriving for centuries after, this stunning collection of pyramids located in the Basin of Mexico was a political and spiritual center when it was in use. Of the many pyramids present was a Temple to Quetzalcoatl (sometimes also called Feathered Serpent Pyramid). On the steps that ascend the pyramid are 260 feathered serpent heads that may have been used as a tracker for the ritual calendar of the unnamed peoples that predated the Aztecs in that area.

② The Dragon Well

Location: Longjing, Hangzhou Province, China

The West Lake of Longjing is renowned for its green tea. With cascading fields down a hill to a large lake, it also boasts a beautiful landscape. The name of the area, Longjing, translates to "Dragon's Well." Local lore states that a magnificent dragon was once summoned by a monk to fill the village well during a particularly gruesome drought, and the name stuck to not only the region, but the exquisite tea it produces.

❖ ❖ ❖

③ Cathedral Notre-Dame de Rouen
Location: Rouen, France

The cathedral of Rouen not only boasts three towers with unique architectural designs, but legend also has it that it is the birthplace of the gargoyle. The French gargouille was a menacing creature that the Rouen townsfolk and clergymen trapped and burnt at the stake. The head, so used to spouting fire, remained pristine no matter how long they burned the rest of the remains. Unable to destroy the head, the people of Rouen placed it atop the church's arches as a reminder to all devilish creatures of the power of God.

④ Hùng King Temple
Location: Ho Chi Minh, Vietnam

This temple venerates the Hông Bàng dynasty, of which the Dragon Lord, Lạc Long Quân is the first patriarch. The temple was built in the 1920s and is nestled in the Saigon Botanical Garden. Dragon motifs are worked into the architecture throughout, and the temple hosts an annual festival honoring the Hống Bàng kings and their Dragon Lord father.

⑤ Guardians of the Ishtar Gate
Location: Babylon, Modern Day Iraq

Ishtar was a goddess of love, sexuality, war, and fertility in Babylonian mythology. Although the Ishtar Gate is fragmented and a ruin now, in its prime, it represented the power and wealth of the early Babylonian empire. A stunning sapphire blue and covered with golden dragons and the aurochs (an extinct animal like a bull), it is believed to have been built between 600 and 500 BCE, possibly earlier.

❖ ❖ ❖

Excavated in the early 1900s by German archaeologists, a recreation constructed with the remnants of the gate is visible in the Pergamon Museum in Berlin. Ishtar Gate replicas are also a common entry way at Iraqi embassies.

⑥ Dragon Head Mountain
Location: Southern Sinai, Egypt
Near the border of where Africa meets the Middle East, towers Makhroum Mountain, a stone dragon head dubbed by tourists as Dragon Head Mountain. The rock formation resembles a large resting dragon skull, complete with a reptilian snout and vacuous eyes. At the right point in the day, the eyes will glow red as burning embers. Its formation and origins are a mystery.

⑦ Sun Gate
Location: Tiwanaku, Bolivia
An archaeological dig site, much like Teotihuacan in Mexico, the Sun Gate is over a millennium old. Either Incan or Andean in origin, the stone arch may have been moved to its current location before it was stumbled upon by European explorers in the 1800s. Stone reliefs of Amaru are etched into the sun gate and the rest of the archaeological site.

⑧ Fire-Breathing Dragons
Location: Lipetsk, Russia
The multi-headed Slavic dragon, Zmey Gorynych, appears in many Slavic and Russian folktales. In one story, a Russian hero chases Zmey into his mountain home after he kidnaps

❖ ❖ ❖

a princess. While the mountain is not specified, it was likely somewhere along the border of the Middle East. Kudykina Gora is a park close to the border and south of Moscow with an enormous, three-headed Zmey Gorynych that actually breathes fire! While we may not be able to identify the exact location of Zmey Gorynych's home, he'd likely appreciate the monument.

DRAGON LAIRS

① Loch Ness
Location: Loch Ness, Scotland

North of the Highlands in Inverness, Scotland is home to a mysterious aquatic creature from Scottish folklore that lurks in the largest loch (by volume) in Scotland. Multiple circumstantial sightings of the creature in modern times led to a cryptozoological (or the pseudoscience surrounding legendary creatures of dubious existence) resurgence. The monster, frequently called Nessie, is often rendered as a type of sea serpent and possesses many dragon-like qualities (see page 103). To this day, promises of being able to spot Nessie in the loch have drawn tourists to Scotland.

② Dragon's Rock
Location: Königswinter, Germany

Drachenfels, which literally means "Dragon's Rock" in German, feels like a place out of a fairytale, complete with a castle in ruins called Burg Drachenfels. Supposedly, it was once home of the fearsome Norse dragon, Fafnir (see page 95). Beneath the castle in a cliffside cave, Fafnir hoarded his treasure and set upon anyone who dare take even a single cup from him.

③ Land Dragons
Location: Moloka'i, Hawaii

Mo'o are enormous dragon-like creatures in Hawaiian mythology. When they die, their bodies petrify and coalesce into the land. Certain ridges, like the Kamalo Ridge in Moloka'i, Hawaii, have a lizard-like etching in their hills, which are believed to be the final resting place for a long-dead mo'o. While they prefer freshwater, they've also been known to make their homes in coral reefs.

④ Lerna's Wetlands
Location: Lerna, Greece

The hydra is a many-headed dragon-like creature from Greek mythology. What are now wetlands in Lerna, Greece, used to be a massive, freshwater lake. The lake was deep, dark, and mirrored the sky, a perfect portal to the Underworld. Early Greeks believed it to be the entrance of the Underworld where the Lernaean Hydra served as guard dog with poisonous breath. Slaying the Hydra was said to be one of the labors of Heracles. If travels to Greece aren't in your future, the Hydra constellation is one of the largest in the night sky, visible between Libra, Centaurus, and Cancer.

⑤ Sacred Spring Garden
Location: Shinsen-en, Kyoto, Japan

Next to Nijō Castle in Kyoto you'll find Shinsen-en, or the Sacred Spring Garden. The garden also has a Japanese Buddhist temple, and dragon motifs can be seen all around the shrine. The rain goddess and Dragon Queen Zennyo

Ryūō supposedly resided in one of the ancient pools. Legend has it that Buddhist monks petitioned by the emperor participated in a contest to coax the Zennyo Ryūō into making rain during times of drought.

⑥ Great Serpent Mound

Location: Adams County, Ohio, United States

A human-made serpentine mound has been slithering across Adams County, Ohio, for centuries. Created either around 300 BCE or 1100 CE, the exact origins and purpose of the mound is unknown. It rests on an ancient meteorite strike area and is over 1,300 feet (396 m) long. The effigy mound resembles burial mounds and could be tied to the solstices.

⑦ Dragon-Made Lake

Location: Chini Lake, Pahang, Malayasia

There are a few accounts of nagas and legendary serpents surrounding this freshwater lake in Malaysia. One story states that the lake was created by a frustrated water spirit that was furious at the human developments being made with no care to its wild domain. The spirit caused ceaseless rainfall for years until the lake was filled up. There's also a story of the lost love of Seri Gumum, a cursed dragon (or naga) princess, who got stuck trying to leave the lake with her beloved as he went to the sea. As the sun rose, Seri Gumum was unable to continue her struggle to chase after her over-enthusiastic partner. Once she laid down and gave up, she slowly turned into an island.

Acknowledgments

Many thanks to all the fantasy creators who continue to keep the magic of dragons alive. Their storied history wouldn't be nearly as fascinating without the wealth of interesting modern takes.

I'd like to offer a deep and heartfelt thanks to Cara Donaldson and the marvelous team at Castle for the opportunity to write about dragons. Working with Kathy McInerney was a treasure.

My utmost gratitude goes out to libraries. They are a wealth of knowledge, and research wouldn't have been possible without them.

An additional thanks to my cherished partner that made sure everything in our nest was kept in order while I consumed books and caffeine in equal measure to write this book.

❖ ❖ ❖

About the Author

Agnes Hollyhock is a lifelong lover of cryptids who lives in a mildly haunted house in Massachusetts. Along with the ghosts, she lives with her beloved animal companions, a cat named Jack and a tarantula named Sally.

❖ ❖ ❖

Resources and References

Bruce, Scott. G., ed., 2021. *Penguin Book of Dragons*. New York: Penguin Random House LLC.

Covarrubias, Miguel. 1954. *The Eagle, the Jaguar, and the Serpent*. New York: Borzoi Book Published By Alfred A. Knopf, Inc.

Fontenrose, Joseph Eddy. 1959. *Python: A Study of Delphic Myth and its Origins*. Berkeley: University of California Press.

Hinnells, John R. 1973. *Persian Mythology*. London: Hamlyn.

Ions, Veronica. 1967. *Indian Mythology*. London: Hamlyn.

Jiankun Sun, Translated by Howard Goldblatt. 2021. *Fantastic Creatures of the Mountains and Seas: A Chinese Classic*. New York: Skyhorse Publishing.

Jones, David E. 2000. *Instinct for Dragons*. Oxfordshire: Routledge.

Liu, Tao Tao. 1995. *Gods and Spirits from Chinese Mythology*. New York: P. Bedrick Books.

Mayor, Adrienne. 2022. *Flying Snakes and Griffen Claws: And Other Classical Myths, Historical Oddities, and Scientific Curiosities*. Princeton: Princeton University Press.

———. 2005. *Fossil Legends of the First Americans*. Princeton: Princeton University Press.

———. 2023. *The First fossil Hunters: Paleontology in Greek and Roman Times*. Princeton: Princeton University Press.

Poignant, Roslyn. 1967. *Oceanic Mythology: The Myths of Polynesia, Mironesia, Melanesia, Australia.* London: Paul Hamlyn.

Rose, Carol. 2000. *Giants, Monsters, and Dragons: An Encyclopedia of Folklore, Legend, and Myth.* New York: W. W. Norton & Company.

Stevenson, Cait. 2021. *How to Slay a Dragon: A Fantasy Hero's Guide to the Real Middle Ages.* New York: Tiller Press.

Wilhelm, Richard and H. Martens, Frederick. 2019. *Chinese Fairy Tales and Legends.* New York: Bloomsbury.

Index

❖ ❖ ❖

❖ ❖ ❖

First published in 2025 by Castle Books, an imprint of The Quarto Group,
142 West 36th Street, 4th Floor, New York, NY 10018, USA
(212) 779-4972 www.Quarto.com

EEA Representation, WTS Tax d.o.o.,
Žanova ulica 3, 4000 Kranj, Slovenia.
www.wts-tax.si

10 9 8 7 6 5 4 3 2 1

ISBN: 978-1-57715-540-9

Digital edition published in 2025
eISBN: 978-0-7603-9698-8

Library of Congress Cataloging-in-Publication Data

Names: Hollyhock, Agnes, author.
Title: Dragons : a handbook of history & lore from basilisks to wyverns / Agnes Hollyhock.
    Other titles: Handbook of history and lore from basilisks to wyverns
Description: New York, NY : Wellfleet Press, 2025. | Includes bibliographical references and
    index. | Summary: "Dragons is your beautifully illustrated guide to these mythical creatures
    and their lore across cultures and centuries"-- Provided by publisher.
Identifiers: LCCN 2025002999 (print) | LCCN 2025003000 (ebook) | ISBN 9781577155409
    | ISBN 9780760396988 (ebook) Subjects: LCSH: Dragons--Folklore. | Dragons--History.
Classification: LCC GR830.D7 H645 2025 (print) | LCC GR830.D7 (ebook) | DDC
    398.24/54--dc23/eng/20250210
LC record available at https://lccn.loc.gov/2025002999
LC ebook record available at https://lccn.loc.gov/2025003000

Group Publisher: Rage Kindelsperger
Editorial Director: Erin Canning
Creative Director: Laura Drew
Managing Editor: Cara Donaldson
Editor: Kathy McInerney
Cover Design: Marisa Kwek
Interior Design: Raine Rath
Interior Illustrations by Raine Rath: 4, 6, 10, 26, 44, 72, 88, 91, 99, 103, 105, 119, 120, 125, 133, 135, 142, 158

Printed in Huizhou, Guangdong, China TT062025